DATE DUE			

GUMDROP BOOKS - Bethany, Missouri

D1505729

THE WAY
PEOPLE
LIVE

Cowboys in the
Old West

by Gail B. Stewart

Lucent Books, P.O. Box 289011, San Diego, CA 92198-9011

Titles in The Way People Live series include:
  Cowboys in the Old West
  Life During the French Revolution
  Life in an Eskimo Village
  Life in the Warsaw Ghetto

Library of Congress Cataloging-in-Publication Data

Stewart, Gail, 1949–
    Cowboys in the Old West / by Gail B. Stewart.
        p.   cm. — (The way people live)
    Includes bibliographical references and index.
    ISBN 1-56006-077-8 (acid-free)
    1. Cowboys—West (U.S.)—History—19th century—Juvenile
literature.   2. West (U.S.)—Social life and customs—Juvenile literature.
I. Title.   II. Series.
    F596.S848   1995
    978'.02—dc20
                                                                    94-32251
                                                                    CIP
                                                                    AC

Copyright 1995 by Lucent Books, Inc., P.O. Box 289011, San Diego, California, 92198-9011

Printed in the U.S.A.

Contents

Discovering the Humanity in Us All

The Way People Live series focuses on pockets of human culture. Some of these are current cultures, like the Eskimos of the Arctic; others no longer exist, such as the Jewish ghetto in Warsaw during World War II. What many of these cultural pockets share, however, is the fact that they have been viewed before, but not completely understood.

To really understand any culture, it is necessary to strip the mind of the common notions we hold about groups of people. These stereotypes are the archenemies of learning. It does not even matter whether the stereotypes are positive or negative; they are confining and tight. Removing them is a challenge that's not easily met, as anyone who has ever tried it will admit. Ideas that do not fit into the templates we create are unwelcome visitors—ones we would prefer remain quietly in a corner or forgotten room.

The cowboy of the Old West is a good example of such confining roles. The cowboy was courageous, yet soft-spoken. His time (it is always a he, in our template) was spent alternatively saving a rancher's daughter from certain death on a runaway stagecoach, or shooting it out with rustlers. At times, of course, he was likely to get a little crazy in town after a trail drive, but for the most part, he was the epitome of inner strength. It is disconcerting to find out that the cowboy is human, even a bit childish. Can it really be true that cowboys would line up to help the cook on the trail drive grind coffee, just hoping he would give them a little stick of pep-

permint candy that came with the coffee shipment? The idea of tough cowboys vying with one another to help "Coosie" (as they called their cooks) for a bit of candy seems silly and out of place.

So is the vision of Eskimos playing video games and watching MTV, living in prefab housing in the Arctic. It just does not fit with what "Eskimo" means. We are far more comfortable with snow igloos and whale blubber, harpoons and kayaks.

Although the cultures dealt with in Lucent's The Way People Live series are often historically and socially well known, the emphasis is on the personal aspects of life. Groups of people, while unquestionably affected by their politics and their governmental structures, are more than those institutions. How do people in a particular time and place educate their children? What do they eat? And how do they build their houses? What kinds of work do they do? What kinds of games do they enjoy? The answers to these questions bring these cultures to life. People's lives are revealed in the particulars and only by knowing the particulars can we understand these cultures' will to survive and their moments of weakness and greatness.

This is not to say that understanding politics does not help to understand a culture. There is no question that the Warsaw ghetto, for example, was a culture that was brought about by the politics and social ideas of Adolf Hitler and the Third Reich. But the Jews who were crowded together in the ghetto cannot be understood by the Reich's politics. Their life was a day-to-day battle for existence, and the creativity and methods they used to prolong their lives is a vital story of human perseverance that would be denied by focusing only on the institutions of Hitler's Germany. Knowing that children as young as five or six outwitted Nazi guards on a daily basis, that Jewish policemen helped the Germans control the ghetto, that children attended secret schools in the ghetto and even earned diplomas—these are the things that reveal the fabric of life, that can inspire, intrigue, and amaze.

Books in the The Way People Live series allow both the casual reader and the student to see humans as victims, heroes, and onlookers. And although humans act in ways that can fill us with feelings of sorrow and revulsion, it is important to remember that "hero," "predator," and "victim" are dangerous terms. Heaping undue pity or praise on people reduces them to objects, and strips them of their humanity.

Seeing the Jews of Warsaw only as victims is to deny their humanity. Seeing them only as they appear in surviving photos, staring at the camera with infinite sadness, is limiting, both to them and to those who want to understand them. To an object of pity, the only appropriate response becomes "Those poor creatures!" and that reduces both the quality of their struggle and the depth of their despair. No one is served by such two-dimensional views of people and their cultures.

With this in mind, the The Way People Live series strives to flesh out the traditional, two-dimensional views of people in various cultures and historical circumstances. Using a wide variety of primary quotations—the words not only of the politicians and government leaders, but of the real people whose lives are being examined—each book in the series attempts to show an honest and complete picture of a culture removed from our own by time or space.

By examining cultures in this way, the reader will notice not only the glaring differences from his or her own culture, but also will be struck by the similarities. For indeed, people share common needs—warmth, good company, stability, and affirmation from others. Ultimately, seeing how people really live, or have lived can only enrich our understanding of ourselves.

An American Fixture

No single group of people in all of American history have more written about them than the cowboys of the Old West. They are glorified in song and in novels. Hollywood has made hundreds of movies about cowboys, complete with fast horses and blazing six-shooters. And some of television's most enduring series have been westerns, with cowboys as their heroes.

A Heroic Image

The image most people have of the cowboy comes from these books, movies, and television shows. The cowboy is a man who frequently engages in fistfights or shootouts with desperadoes, battles Indian war parties, and, with the aid of his lightning-fast horse, saves runaway stagecoaches.

A movie still from The Magnificent Seven *depicts the common idea of the cowboy—rugged, handsome, and full of mystery.*

No Rival for the American Cowboy

In the preface to his book The Real American Cowboy, *Jack Weston explains how deeply the image of the heroic cowboy is embedded in the American culture.*

"My point is that the popular cowboy hero has lasted a long time and has pervaded every corner of our culture. I can't think of a rival for the cowboy as the most important of our popular heroes, if by that we mean the generic national types, composed of hundreds of individuals in the media. The cowboy is the most durable, the most influential, and the most varied to accommodate our differences and contradictions. Here is a random list of national heroes during the present century: the frontier explorer or mountain man, the pioneer settler, the rags-to-riches business genius, the tough private eye, the GI, the gangster, the fearless newspaper editor, the movie star or entertainer, the on-the-road poet-philosopher, the world-weary expatriate of the Lost Generation, the misunderstood and brooding teenager, the populist politician or organizer, the major league baseball player, the prizefighter, the selfless nurse. (I can't help remarking in passing that this almost all-male list shows how sexist our culture is.) One might question one or another of the types, but no one would deny that the cowboy, in his changing forms, has entered more deeply into the consciousness of more Americans of different generations and backgrounds than any of the popular types I've listed or any I've forgotten."

He is in love with the wide-open spaces of the West and is at home sleeping under the stars, with only his trusty horse for company. He is resourceful and intelligent in the ways of nature—although he may not have had much "book learnin'." And though this cowboy is a heroic figure, he remains humble and gentle—and always soft-spoken. Writer Russell Freedman learned as a young boy that a cowboy was "a fellow who says 'yup' and 'nope,' who never complains, who shoots straight, and whose horse comes when he whistles."[1]

Although these images are romantic and even tender, they are not totally accurate. As tempting as it might be to cast the American cowboy in such a glamorous, heroic role, say historians, it's important to keep in mind that he was—above all else—a laborer. One expert, William W. Savage Jr., offers a reality check:

The cowboy, it must be remembered, was a hired hand, employed to tend cattle, whether on range or trail, and his work was strenuous and dirty, his hours were long, and his pay was minimal. Cowboying required no particular skills beyond the initial ability to sit on a horse and pay attention. . . . The work was simply more tiring than heroic, more boring than romantic.[2]

"Doesn't Sound Much Like Cowboys"

Others agree that many of the traits associated with the cowboy are false. To learn about the real American cowboy, they say, one must strip away all the untruths created by movies and fiction.

The silent, tough-guy image, for one, seems to have been invented by Hollywood. Historian Jack Weston points out that many of the cowboys had been southern farmers, and the pastimes and activities they enjoyed on the range reflected that earlier occupation:

> They would have wrestling contests while they waited for supper. They would listen to the music of fiddle, mouth organ, or banjo (seldom guitar, which was Mexican), music played by one of their number or the cook. The tunes would be things like "Billy in the Low Ground," "Dinah Had a Wooden Leg," "The Devil's Dream," "Sally Gooden," "Arkansas Traveler," and "Give the Fiddler a Dram [shot of liquor]."

> They would take the endgate off the chuck wagon, lay it on the ground, and one cowboy would noisily dance a jig on it with his high-heeled boots while the rest would clap in time. . . . Doesn't sound much like cowboys.[3]

Encouraging the Myths

For most of the American people who resided in the cities and villages of the East, the life of the cowboy seemed glorious and free. Some people had heard tales of savage Indian tribes and the dangers encountered on long cattle drives. They had also heard stories of the wild activities of the cowboys when they reached the end of the drive—drinking and gambling in saloons.

Perhaps because they enjoyed being thought of as wild and rough, many young cowboys encouraged the image. They frequently scared visitors to the West, sometimes brandishing pistols and even staging mock holdups. And many cowboys posed for photographers in various trail towns, using studio "props" to achieve the desired effect. Writes one historian:

> [With] Colts, Winchesters, and Bowie knives, always prominently displayed; cartridge belts, . . . fancy shirts and bandannas, saddles slung over papier-mâché rocks, rawhide [lariats] held menacingly

Cowboys burst into a hotel in this painting by Charles M. Russell. After being away for months on a cattle drive, cowboys came into town ready to have some fun.

"A Round of Boisterous Gaiety"

The character of the cowboy was much discussed in the cow towns of Kansas during the 1860s and 1870s. There was something mysterious about him—a fascinating combination of pomposity and earthiness, as quoted by the editor of the Topeka Commonwealth *on August 15, 1871—included in Don Worcester's book* The Chisholm Trail: High Road of the Cattle Kingdom.

"The Texas cattle herder is a character, the like of which can be found nowhere else on earth. Of course he is unlearned and illiterate, with but few wants and meager ambition. His diet is principally navy plug and whiskey and the occupation dearest to his heart is gambling. His dress consists of a flannel shirt with a handkerchief encircling his neck, butternut pants and a pair of long boots, in which are always the legs of his pants. His head is covered by a sombrero, which is a Mexican hat with a high crown and a brim of enormous dimensions. He generally wears a revolver on each side of his person, which he will use with as little hesitation on a man as on a wild animal. Such a character is dangerous and desperate and each one has generally killed

When cowboys went into town, professional photographers often asked them to pose for pictures to use on postcards and other memorabilia.

his man. . . . They drink, swear, and fight, and life with them is a round of boisterous gaiety and indulgence in sensual pleasure."

as if they were weapons . . . they would look particularly tough, occasionally with a cigarette or cigar slanting down from the corner of their mouths.[4]

"We Was the Salt of the Earth"

But stripping away the myth from the reality of the American cowboy does not make him

uninteresting—far from it! Even without the exaggerations, his occupation was difficult and dangerous. Eighteen-hour days in the saddle were not uncommon. And even though gunplay was the exception rather than the rule, there was danger from outlaws, as well as from Native Americans and white settlers intent on maintaining the land as it was.

The era of the cowboy was astonishingly short—approximately twenty-five years.

Between the end of the Civil War and 1890, however, some eight million head of cattle were herded—by means of long trail drives—from Texas to Kansas and points north, and shipped to market. The difficulty and danger of the work was a source of pride to the thousands of cowboys who worked the range during that time. One cowboy remembered being "a totally different class from the other fellows on the frontier. We was the salt of the earth, anyway in our estimation, and we had the pride that went with it."[5]

Who were these men? What was it really like to be a cowboy in the days of the great trail drives from Texas to Kansas? What was it about the cowboy that made him more intriguing to America than loggers, explorers, farmers, railroad workers, and others who made their living in the expanding West? What was it about their lives that captured and held the imaginations of the American people as no other single group of workers had?

The Roots of the American Cowboy

To really understand the American cowboy of the Old West, it is first necessary to look at the business in which he played a key role. Interestingly, the herding and transport of cattle in North America was not invented by the nineteenth-century American cowboy. On the contrary, the business of tending cattle had been going on in North America for more than three hundred years.

Coming from Spain

Cattle are not native to the Americas. They first arrived with Columbus, on his second voyage to the New World. Along with the supplies and materials necessary to establish a Spanish settlement—farm tools, seeds, chickens, and goats—were horses and cattle. The Spanish colonists who arrived with Columbus were intending to bring the best of their country to this new, unknown land.

Much prized by the Spaniards were the hardy and muscular cattle they raised in the south of Spain for two important purposes—food and bullfights. The animals' long, razor-sharp horns and surly dispositions were clear signals that they were well suited for the bullring. In their new environment, however, the weather was warm, the rivers and streams sparkled with fresh water, and the prairie

Spaniards unload the first cattle in North America at Veracruz, Mexico. Without cattle, there could be no cowboy.

The vaqueros *were excellent horsemen and tenders of cattle, and often amused themselves with contests and games that showed off their skills. In his book* Cowboys and Cattle Country, *Don Ward describes some of the games played by the* vaqueros, *some of which would be considered cruel by today's standards.*

"Vaqueros and their masters occupied what leisure time they had with games of skill that derived from their work. One of their favorite sports was called *corrida de toro*. A lively bull was let loose within a fenced arena and mounted men waved capes or *serapes* at him until he charged. He was chased by all the riders, each one trying to *colear el toro*— to grasp his tail and give it a twist that would dump him to the ground.

Another game [they] played was to rope a grizzly bear—three or four vaqueros worked together to get several lariats onto a big one—and then to match the bear in a gory, eye-popping fight with the strongest, fiercest bull rounded up at the rodeo. Horse racing and roping contests were popular sports, and there were various riding tricks. One required a horseman to lean low from the saddle while riding at top speed and scoop up a coin from the ground. In another, a coin was placed beneath each knee of the rider, who then galloped and jumped his mount over several hurdles and, returning over the same course, wove in and out among the hurdles to halt before a judge who checked to see that the coins were still in place.

A live rooster was roughly used in a game called *el carrera del gallo*. The bird was buried in the dirt with only his head showing. Starting from two hundred feet away, a vaquero spurred to a gallop, and as he rode by, leaned from the saddle and tried to grab the rooster by the neck and pull him free."

grasses were lush and green. No land could have been more favorable for these transplanted cattle, and the small herd from Spain flourished.

In Spain ranchers had kept their livestock in pens. In the New World, it was not necessary to worry about animals wandering off. There was nowhere on the great grassy plains for animals to hide, nowhere for them to get lost. The Spanish settlers happily let the cattle roam free.

In a very short time, the herds multiplied—historians say that every fifteen months their numbers doubled. In 1540, when the explorer Coronado prepared a caravan to accompany him in his search for gold, he reportedly had no difficulty assembling a herd of five hundred cattle. And thirty years later, a visitor to Mexico wrote in his journal of ranches "stretching endlessly and everywhere covered with an infinite number of cattle."

By the seventeenth century, a herd of fewer than 20,000 was considered quite small. It was not uncommon for Spanish settlers in Mexico to have 150,000 or more. As one witness wrote, "[Cattle] were being born and multiplying unbelievably; you cannot exaggerate their numbers or imagine the spectacle before your eyes."[6]

The First Cowboys

Even though most ranchers in the 1600s continued to let their huge herds roam free, the cattle still had to be looked after throughout the year. Calves needed to be branded for purposes of identification, and cows had to be doctored when sick or calving. When it was slaughtering time, someone had to capture the cattle and kill them. And because there were so many cattle grazing on the open range, cattle theft was on the increase. The Spaniards had to be sure that the herds were watched closely.

The Spanish ranchers, however, considered themselves far too important to spend their time tending cattle. Instead, they gave the job to slaves: young Aztec men who had been captured when the Spanish first came to Mexico. These prisoners were made to do jobs that were difficult, dirty, or unpleasant. Tending the cattle herds was one of these jobs.

The first of the herders had something in common with the cattle they managed: they were branded. Just as cows are marked with a red-hot iron, newly captured slaves were marched in lines past bonfires. "As each man's turn came," writes one historian, "a blacksmith drew a branding iron from the fire and burned the letter *G* for *guerra*, 'war,' on his lips and cheeks."[7]

For many years a herder—known as a *vaquero*, from *vaca*, the Spanish word for

What to Bring

In his book Cowboy Culture: A Saga of Five Centuries, *David Dary quotes a letter written in the early 1830s by two settlers in Texas, which was then part of Mexico. They were writing to tell friends back in the United States what sorts of things they needed to bring if they wanted to come set up a ranch in Texas.*

"Bring some boxes of glass, bars soap, plenty wick, bring seeds of every kind, shallots; bring cross cut, whip, and frame saws. . . . Bring as many cart wheels and cart mountings as you can, chains for oxen; no timber, as this is the country for timber of every kind. Bring a supply of sugar coffee and tea and flour for 8 or 9 months; if you have any to spare, you can get your price. Gun locks and everything belonging to locks, screws of every kind, plates for screws. Your goods both small and large and every little article you can pack. Pots, pans with covers, oven etc., white muslin both white and brown in pieces. Bring tin cups. Porringers. Any man working 2 days in the week may take his gun and fishing rod the remainder and his horse. Bring your clean English blankets both secondhand and new. . . . Bring a candle mould. . . . Bring your beds, you'll have no work, your daughters can milk 50 cows for you, and make butter which is 25 cents a pound here. . . . A cow has 2 calves in 10 months. . . . The healthiest country in the world."

Vaqueros *round up longhorn cattle in Mexico. Such a job was difficult and dangerous, as the longhorn cattle were half-wild and often tried to gore the* vaquero *and his horse.*

cow—did his work from the ground. He carried a staff, much like a shepherd, and often had a few dogs to help him. Even so, the work was impossibly difficult. The herds were so vast that many of the cattle had been running wild their whole lives and had never set eyes on a human being. Fear of humans made the animals vicious, especially the big bulls. They charged the young *vaqueros* and swung their sharp horns at both the men and the herding dogs. Even the young calves were a problem. Although not aggressive, they stubbornly refused to be separated from the herd at branding time—capturing a single calf might take a man on foot several hours.

Rising to the Backs of Horses

It was not that the Spaniards were ignorant to the advantages of horseback riding—far from it. The Spanish were among the finest horsemen in the world. The sturdy little horses

they had brought from Spain were lively and fast, and highly prized by the ranchers, who rode for pleasure as well as for transportation.

But riding mounted on a horse was not an activity for slaves. The ranchers, as well as other Spanish settlers, felt very strongly that there were important differences between themselves and the native population, who were thought of as inferior in intelligence, and untrustworthy. To let such people ride horses might give the slaves the impression that they were the equals of their masters, and that would not do. As one historian writes, "The equestrian life was reserved for 'decent people'; it was too dangerous and democratic to let nonwhites rise up from the ground to mount a horse."[8]

As the size of the herds ballooned over the years, however, it no longer made sense to expect the *vaqueros* to do their work on foot. The ranchers taught their slaves to ride—and what a world was opened up to the *vaqueros*! "They took to the saddle easily, gaily, for riding brought self-respect," one historian writes. "A horseman, however poor, was a proud person. He rose above the crowd, who ate his dust as he galloped past."[9]

Dressing for the Job

Being a *vaquero* was both difficult and dangerous. It is not surprising, therefore, that a man who held the job was eager to make any changes necessary in keeping himself safe and comfortable while he worked. Even the clothing he wore was chosen with those things in mind.

His hat was called a *sombrero*—"shade maker" in Spanish. It had a low, flat crown and a straight brim. A sombrero might be made of leather, felt, or woven palm fiber—it

The patron of the ranch made sure that both he and his horse were outfitted in a style that showed their prominent status.

made no difference as long as it protected the *vaquero* from the hot Mexican sun.

Most *vaqueros* wore shirts and vests of leather, which was abundant on the ranches and had the advantage of being both waterproof and wind resistant. The same applied to the long pants they wore, called *chaparejos*. Used by the American cowboys years later, these pants became known as "chaps." In their modified, modern form, they are useful in protecting the legs from constant rubbing against the bumps and buckles of the saddle, and from rough brush and other vegetation.

Boots were not a part of the *vaquero*'s wardrobe, not because they would not have been useful, but because they were worn only by the Spanish ranchers. "It would have been a rare *vaquero* who could afford the expensive boots worn by wealthy Spaniards, which were made of the finest cordovan and morocco leathers," writes one historian. "Such boots were exceedingly wide at the top, often lined with silk or velvet, and made to be worn with silk stockings, something few if any *vaqueros* owned."[10] Instead of boots, most cattle herders were barefoot, or if they wore shoes at all, they wore sandals.

The *vaqueros*' lack of footwear did not keep them from wearing an important piece of equipment—iron spurs. The business end of a spur was a sharp rotating disk called a rowel. The rowels were very large—often eight inches in diameter—and were needed to penetrate the thick hair to prod the horses. They were attached to sandals or bare feet, and as historian David Dary writes, were a source of pride even though they were often cumbersome:

> The large rowels made walking very difficult, but then the *vaquero* never walked when he could ride. . . . When

a *vaquero* did walk, the rubbing heel chains attached to the rowel pin—these were later to be called jinglebobs—gave off a bright ringing sound. To the *vaquero*, the spurs were a badge of his calling."[11]

Doing Their Jobs

Because the herds were large and there were so many wild cattle, *vaqueros* on many ranches decided to set aside regular times for herding the cattle from one spot to another. These

Knightlike, a vaquero *proudly carries the twelve-foot pole that he will use to slaughter cattle. First, the crescent-shaped head was used to sever a leg tendon, then to sever the spinal cord.*

roundups were called *rodeos*, after the Spanish word meaning "to surround." The rodeos, held every two weeks or so, gave the *vaqueros* a chance to check for unmarked cattle, or to sort their own from other ranchers'. Rodeos also accustomed the cattle to being handled by humans.

Slaughtering was a big part of the *vaquero*'s job, since cattle were killed by the thousands—both for their hides and for tallow, or fat. The hides were leather for saddles, clothing, and scores of other uses. The tallow could be eaten, made into either soap or candles. There were so many cattle that it took only a tiny fraction of the herd to keep the rancher and his workers well fed. Thus most of the cattle killed were not used as meat.

Cattle earmarked for slaughter were killed out in the open, right on the prairie. The *vaquero* used a half-moon-shaped knife on the end of a twelve-foot pole, which he carried much like a jousting knight. He rode close to his target, then thrust the knife forward until the cow's hind leg struck the knife's sharp edge. Writer David Dary explains:

> As the animal's large tendon was cut, it became helpless and fell to the ground. The *vaquero* then dismounted and drove one end of the knife into the animal's head just behind the horns, severing the spinal cord. Once the animal was dead, the hide was removed and pegged out on the ground to dry.[12]

The process, known later as "hamstringing," was very easy for the herders. So easy was it, in fact, that many *vaqueros* killed far more cattle than were needed for meat, tallow, or hides. Carcasses were left to rot in the fields, victims of *vaqueros* who had used their sharp knives to kill for sport, or to make a

A Mexican vaquero *brands cattle. Cattle branding was an important part of the cowboy's work.*

little extra money, as one historian wrote. The *vaqueros*, he claimed, "acquired such dexterity that to amuse themselves or to sell hides—sometimes without consulting the livestock owners—they decimated [killed large portions of] the herds."[13]

The rope, or la reata, *was an important piece of equipment for the cowboy, who used it to rope the half-wild cattle while still staying astride his horse.*

La Reata

As years went by, an organization of ranchers in Mexico banned hamstringing, for too many cattle were being slaughtered needlessly. A new tool evolved for the *vaqueros*, one that was not cruel like the moon-shaped knife had been. This new tool took far more skill to use correctly, but in time it proved to be the herders' most important piece of equipment.

It was called *la reata*—the rope with a loop at the end. Thrown over the horns of a cow, or the neck of a wild horse, the rope could hold the animal securely so that the *vaquero* could do his work—branding, doctoring wounds, or preparing animals for slaughter. The rope was anywhere from 65 to 110 feet long, and as thick as a man's little finger. It was woven from four strips of rawhide, or in some cases, strands of horsehair.

The idea of using *la reata* was fairly simple. The *vaquero* would lasso, or throw the rope around, an animal. He then would wrap his end of the rope around something to keep up the tension. Eventually, saddles

Improving Saddles

Many of the vaqueros *rode bareback; others used crudely constructed saddles which were little better than blankets lashed together with rawhide thongs. In David Dary's book* Cowboy Culture: A Saga of Five Centuries, *he quotes a writer from the mid-1800s who describes the improvements made by California saddle makers.*

No cowboy could do his job without a saddle. Its features slowly improved to increase the cowboy's stability on the horse.

"When strapped on, it rests so firmly in position that the strongest pull of a horse upon a lariat attached to the pommel can not displace it. Its shape is such that the rider is compelled to sit nearly erect, with his legs on the continuation of the line of the body, which makes his seat more secure, and, at the same time, gives him a better control over his arms and horse. The position is attained by setting the stirrup-leathers farther back than on the old-fashioned saddle. The pommel is high, like the Mexican saddle, and prevents the rider from being thrown forward. The tree is covered with raw hide, put on green, and sewed; when this dries and contracts it gives it great strength. It has no iron in its composition, but is kept together by buckskin strings, and can easily be taken to pieces for mending or cleaning. It has a hair girth about five inches wide. The whole saddle is covered with a large and thick sheet of sole-leather, having a hole to lay over the pommel; it extends back over the horse's hips, and protects them from rain, and when taken off in camp it furnishes a good security against dampness when placed under the traveler's bed. The California saddle-tree is regarded by many as the best of all others for the horse's back, and as having an easier seat than the Mexican."

adapted to roping were constructed with a knob in the front for this purpose. However, the first *vaqueros* to use such ropes braided one end into their horses' tails—a method that made some onlookers wince. One man who witnessed this style of roping bulls was shocked:

> I never could believe this till I saw it. It always struck me that it would either pull the horse's tail out by the root, or else throw him down; and so it would, but the horses become so cunning and so fond of the sport, that the moment the lasso leaves the hand of the rider, instead of stopping short, as I always imagined was the method, they gallop off at a slight tangent [angle] as fast as they can, when if the lasso is round the leg, the slightest jerk brings the bull to the ground.[14]

No matter how the rope was anchored, the *vaqueros* showed a real artistry in their ability to throw *la reata*. They developed several types of loop—one for catching the legs of a running animal, another for catching the front legs only, a third for looping around the neck of a wild horse. Their accuracy was legendary. One *vaquero* was said to be able to lasso an eagle in flight!

Pushing North

The skills of the *vaquero* were crucial to the expansion of the Spanish settlers in Mexico. Wherever new villages were established, it was necessary to move herds, too, for people needed a ready food supply. When silver was discovered in what is now northern Mexico, *vaqueros* drove thousands of cattle north, where mines were dug and staffed with workers. And in the early 1700s the *vaqueros*

and their cattle crossed the Rio Grande into what is now the state of Texas, maintaining herds there.

Throughout the next hundred years there were bloody battles in Texas as ownership of the land changed hands—from the Spanish, to the Mexicans, who wanted independence from Spanish rule, to settlers from the United States. The activity on the land remained the same, however. Vast herds of cattle, maintained by men on horseback, continued to roam the open range. And although the day of the Spanish ranchers in Texas was all but over, the *vaqueros* had a great influence on the North American cowboys who came after them.

Not only did the Americans learn the *vaqueros'* skills of roping and riding, they took over many of the Spanish words used in herding. *La reata* became "lariat." The leather pants called *chaparejos* became the cowboys' "chaps." Even the word *vaquero* changed into "buckaroo"—another term for a cowboy.

A Long Way to Market

The Spanish longhorns continued to thrive on the Texas prairie, although American ranchers who came west brought cattle of their own, too. The herds multiplied quickly, for the Texas prairie was as fertile as the land south of the Rio Grande had been hundreds of years before.

The American ranchers raised cattle for the same reasons the Mexicans and the Spanish had. Some were slaughtered for beef, but the majority were killed for hides, tallow, and the hooves and horns, which were processed into glue.

People in other parts of America would have welcomed the good-tasting beef being

Vaqueros drive cattle on a Texas hacienda. Although the days of the powerful *hacienda owners drew to a close, the* vaquero *continued to play a vital role.*

raised in Texas, but the problems in getting the cattle to the nearest market, at least a thousand miles away, were enormous. Railroads were beginning to push their way westward in the mid-1800s, but not nearly as far as Texas. It would be many years before ranchers could send their cattle to eastern markets via rail.

Even so, some Texans tried to drive their herds to markets. In 1842 there was a cattle drive to New Orleans. It was extremely difficult, for the herds had to cross through swampland, and many were lost in the process. Another rancher, W.H. Snyder, organized a drive to California in 1849. Gold had recently been discovered, and miners by the hundreds were pouring into the area. Snyder knew that any cattle he could get to California would be eagerly bought by the hungry miners.

That drive was difficult, too. The cattle were moved across Texas, through parts of the present states of Wyoming, Utah, and Nevada, and on to San Francisco. It took nearly two years, and many cattle died from cold, from heat, and from exhaustion. Even so, when Snyder arrived, he was paid the unbelievably high price of $125 per head—more than five times what he invested in the drive.

Encouraged by Snyder's success, other ranchers tried the same thing during the 1850s. However, few had the good fortune of the Snyder expedition. Indian tribes, hostile because the cattle were being driven through their land, made attacks on the cowboys and cattle. Sometimes, to avoid lands where Indians might be waiting to attack, cattle drivers took their herds through deserts, where many cattle died for lack of water. "Herds crossed stretches of desert," writes one historian, "leaving behind dead cattle to become mounds of bleached bones. You could see them for miles, glittering snow-white in the sun."[15]

Stampeding down Third Avenue

The most adventurous of the early cattle drives took place in 1854. Two enterprising men, Tom Candy Ponting and Washington Malone, rode from Illinois to Texas to buy six hundred head of cattle. They knew the biggest market would be New York City, and they knew if they could get a herd all the way there, they would be rich.

Like their predecessors in the westward cattle drives, Ponting and Malone had to cross Indian lands in Kansas and Missouri. They and their herd also had to negotiate treacherous rivers, swollen with spring rains. In addition, there was the constant fear that something would startle the herd and Ponting and Malone would be unable to hold them. "I was so afraid that something would scare the cattle," wrote Ponting in his journal, "that I could not sleep in the tent."[16]

The herd reached Illinois, where many of the cattle were sold. Ponting and Malone took 150 of the best cattle and headed east to New York City. The journey was twenty-one hundred miles, and the most interesting part was the excitement caused by driving the entire herd down Third Avenue to the livestock market on Twenty-fourth Street. In those days New Yorkers were used to seeing animals brought to market—but these scary-looking longhorns were something else again.

"They stampeded," writes one historian, "overflowing the sidewalks and clearing them of pedestrians. Panic swept Third Avenue

as mothers grabbed youngsters and pulled them indoors. Grown men ran for their lives, a few slipping in the muddy, manure-filled streets."[17]

Even though the cattle seemed fierce and wild, the New York newspapers reported with disdain how thin and rangy they looked. One editorial claimed that the cattle "were barely able to cast a shadow." Another newspaper said the cattle "would not weigh anything were it not for their horns, which were useful also in preventing them from crawling through fences."[18]

No one knows whether the difficulties in such long cattle drives could have been made more manageable, for in April 1861 there was an interruption in the cattle business. The Civil War broke out, and President Lincoln declared that there would be no commerce—no trading of any sort—between the North and the South. Most Texans abandoned their farms and ranches and joined the Confederacy; their herds were left to wander untended.

Starting Again

When the war ended in 1865, the ranchers returned home. The South had surrendered, and the people were weary of war and without much hope. Their once-strong economy was in shambles. Confederate money, with its likeness of Confederate president Jefferson Davis, was worthless. To make matters worse, it didn't seem likely that the defeated southerners would soon begin earning any U.S. currency. All they had of value were the nearly six million cattle that still roamed the open range.

Ranchers knew that in Texas the cattle were worth only about $3 a head for tallow, horns, and hooves. On the other hand, each

Lincoln visits Union troops during the Civil War. Many ranchers and vaqueros *abandoned their cattle on the range to fight in the war.*

animal would bring $40 in the East, if the herds could be transported to market somehow. So in the months following the Civil War, Texas ranchers busied themselves with plans to get their herds to market. The railroad system had expanded, with track laid as far as Kansas, north of Texas, and the idea seemed less far-fetched than it had before the war. It would be difficult driving cattle such a long way, and there would surely be risks involved. Ranchers in Missouri and Kansas, worried about the disease-bearing ticks many longhorns carried, would fight to keep Texas cattle out. There would be rustlers, hostile Native Americans, deserts without water, and a host of other dangers. Besides, the trail drives would be time-consuming, with no guarantee of success.

But, as one historian remarked, "these Texans had plenty of time, and there was an old range saying that nobody ever drowned himself in sweat."[19] Besides, it was not the ranchers who would be doing the driving of the herds. That job would be left to the young men arriving at ranches all over Texas each day looking for work—the cowboys.

2 The Masters of the Range

Texas ranchers were not the only ones looking for ways to earn money after the Civil War. Hundreds of youths—some of them still boys—came to Texas after the war as word of the new cattle business spread. These young men owned neither cattle nor land, but they were willing to work for the ranchers as hired hands.

"Faceless Youths on Horseback"

The "faceless youths on horseback," as one cowboy later described them, came from a variety of backgrounds. Many were Texans, or natives of other southern states, returning from defeat in the Confederate army. Because of the floundering postwar economy in the South, jobs were scarce. Rounding up cattle and driving them to market often seemed like a good prospect for these young men, many of whom, say historians, were anxious to work off a little steam from their frustrating war experiences.

But not all the men looking for work as cowboys were former Confederate soldiers. There were men from Illinois, Ohio, Wisconsin, and other northern states who had fought in the Union army but, now that the war was over, were in no hurry to return home. They were from little towns and quiet farms that seemed frightfully dull after years of combat. These young men were looking for adventure, and the West had a growing reputation for being wild and untamed.

And although cowboys are nearly always portrayed in movies and on television as white, there were substantial numbers of minorities, too. Many Mexican men, descendants of the *vaqueros*, were eager to sign on as cowboys in the growing cattle business. Black men, too—former slaves who had worked on cattle ranches or on the cotton plantations of east Texas. Now that slavery was abolished, plantations could no longer function as before, and the possibilities for employment in the South were scarce. About one-third of the men looking for work on Texas ranches were black or Mexican.

"From Every Land"

Not all the cowboys were Americans. Theodore Roosevelt, who spent time on a ranch in North Dakota learning to rope and ride, wrote in his memoirs, "Cowboys are from every land, yet [the foreigners] soon become indistinguishable from their American companions. . . . All have a certain curious similarity . . . existence in the West seems to put the same stamp on each."[20]

Some of the newcomers were Scottish, Irish, or German. There were a surprisingly high number of well-educated young British gentlemen who had gotten into trouble back in England, perhaps for criminal behavior or because of alcohol abuse. These young men had one thing in common. They were "the ne'er-do-well offspring of titled families . . .

Black cowboy Nat Love. After the Civil War, some former black slaves became cowboys.

centage could neither read nor write. After all, they reasoned, why did a cowboy need such knowledge? As one Texan later recalled (half-jokingly), "Well, when I got so I could draw a cow and mark a few brands on the slate, I figured I was getting too smart to stay in school."[22]

"Just a Plain Bowlegged Human"

Although they came from a wide variety of backgrounds, cowboys were alike in one respect—they were thin. A fat man placed far too much stress on a horse's back to be worth keeping on the payroll. One observer noted that the hot sun and wind of the range—in addition to the difficulty and excitement of their lives—gave all cowboys a weathered, lined appearance: "Sinewy, hardy, self-reliant, their life forces them to be both daring and adventurous, and the passing over their heads of a few years leaves printed on their faces certain lines which tell of dangers quietly fronted and hardships uncomplainingly endured."[23]

Another, less attractive, sign of the cowboy's craft was noted by one old-time cowboy. He described himself modestly as "just a plain bowlegged human who smells very horsey at times."[24] Cowboys disliked walking and rode whenever possible, but this constant molding their legs around a horse, with the heels always pointed down, changed the shape of their legs. When a cowboy had to walk, he looked a little like a sailor on shore after a long sea voyage.

One cowboy recalled a friend whom he called "dear old Wedding Ring Charlie." Given the name because the lower half of his body had become almost circular from his years in the saddle, Charlie "though ever

[ordered] to stay [in America] until they either disappeared or straightened up."[21] They were called "remittance men," after the sums of money (remittances) sent by their families to get them started in their new lives.

Cowboys who were highly educated were in the minority, however. Most of the men had had little formal education; a high per-

The True Character of a Cowboy

Theodore Roosevelt spent a great deal of time with cowboys when he lived on a Dakota ranch in the 1880s. In his book Ranch Life and the Hunting Trail, *he wrote about the character of cowboys, and how they are misunderstood by outsiders. This passage from Roosevelt's book is quoted in Lon Tinkle's and Allen Maxwell's anthology* The Cowboy Reader.

"No man travelling through or living in the country need fear molestation from the cowboys unless he himself accompanies them on their drinking bouts, or in other ways plays the fool, for they are, with us at any rate, very good fellows, and the most determined and effective foes of real lawbreakers, such as horse and cattle thieves, murderers, etc. Few of the outrages quoted in Eastern papers as their handiwork are such in reality, the average Easterner apparently considering every individual who wears a broad hat and carries a six-shooter a cowboy. These outrages are, as a rule, the work of the roughs and criminals who always gather on the outskirts of civilization, and who infest every frontier town until the decent citizens become sufficiently numerous and determined to take the law into their own hands and drive them out. . . .

The moral tone of a cow camp, indeed, is rather high than otherwise. Meanness, cowardice, and dishonesty are not tolerated. There is a high regard for truthfulness and keeping one's word, intense contempt for any kind of hypocrisy, and a hearty dislike for a man who shirks his work. Many of the men gamble and drink, but many do neither; and the conversation is not worse than in most bodies composed wholly of male human beings. A cowboy will not submit tamely to an insult, and is ever ready to avenge his own wrongs; nor has he an overwrought fear of shedding blood."

In this illustration from Theodore Roosevelt's book, two cowboys keep out of the way of flying hoofs while attempting to "break" a bronco. The horses a cowboy rode were often taken from the wild herds that roamed freely throughout the West.

A cowboy seems to glare defiantly ahead in this painting by Frederick Remington. It was partly the cowboy's desire for independence and a solitary life that drove him to choose his lifestyle.

able firmly to sit his saddle through twenty-four consecutive hours, could only with greatest difficulty walk for twenty yards."[25]

Private People

Besides physical characteristics, many cowboys had certain traits in common. One of these was a wish to keep to themselves. There was a saying in the Old West that none came

there "save for health, wealth, or a ruined reputation." Many young men who came looking for work were "on the dodge" from the law for one reason or another. It was considered bad manners among cowboys to inquire about a person's background—or even his name.

One cowboy recalls that when he was a boy, a stranger had come by the family house. "We ate dinner and then I joined my older brother in asking the stranger what his name was. 'Jones is the name,' he said. As soon as he rode off," writes the cowboy, "our mother laid us boys out for being so ill-mannered as to ask any man his name."[26]

Another cowboy recalls being given some good advice when he had innocently asked the real name of a man who went by the name of Hen. An old ranch hand approached him and said:

> Say, stranger, let me give you some advice. You're a pilgrim. Excuse me, that there just means that you're new to this country. If I was you, I wouldn't try to hurry nothin', and I'd travel on the idee [idea] that Hen likely gave a first-class funeral to the rest of his names, and I wouldn't ask him for no resurrections.[27]

Perhaps for the reason of privacy, or perhaps just for the fun of it, nicknames were given to almost every cowboy. Few created their own—often the name was one the cowboy might not like, but he had little to do with it. Once a name like "One-Tooth" or "Mean Spike" was handed to a man, it usually stuck. "Each section of the Range had its Shorty, Slim, Skinny, Fatty, Squint, or Red as prefix to Bill or Jack or Brown or Smith," writes one historian, "its Texas Joe, Arizona Kid, and Missouri Jim; its Cat's Eye, Hair-Lip, Freckles, or whatever as a prefix to Riley, Jones, or White."[28]

"Cowboy-ese"

Even though many cowboys were private men, reluctant to discuss their personal backgrounds, they enjoyed conversation about other things. On the trail, in the bunkhouse with other cowboys—at times like these they could talk about the job, other ranches they had seen, and people they had worked with.

Cowboys seemed to have a language all their own—a colorful mixture of slang and profanity. The words they used came from a variety of sources besides standard English. From the jargon of gamblers, they used phrases like "a busted flush" (plans gone awry) and "it's high, low, jack, and the game," to signify that a task had been successfully accomplished.

They used a hefty supply of Spanish words, learned from their close contact with Mexican *vaqueros*. Words like *hombre* (man), *pronto* (right away), and *mañana* (tomorrow) were frequently used, as well as the everyday words for cowboy equipment and attire (sombrero, corral, lariat) borrowed from the *vaqueros*.

Cowboys used words like "killikinic" (tobacco) and "skookum" (great), which were borrowed from various Native American languages. Many cowboys even employed hand signals from Indian sign languages when talking to one another—as one historian claims, "to dress up a light-hearted conversation."[29]

Variety was a necessary ingredient to "cowboy-ese." There were plenty of words and phrases the cowboy used to say the same thing. As one historian writes:

Cowboys gather at mealtime. The cowboy's life was one of solitude. When out on a drive, cowboys saw no one but each other for months.

If you were not in a hurry, you "ambled," "jogged," or "moseyed along." But if the Comanche were coming, or the herd stampeded, you would "git," "vamoose," "light out," "burn the earth," "hit the breeze," and "rattle your hocks." If safety wasn't "two whoops and a holler" away, you "turned your toes to the daisies."[30]

"Git" was a trademark of the American cowboy. He used the word as a last resort, when it was important for someone to leave quickly, or for an animal to move without delay. Throughout the Old West, it was understood that when a cowboy used the word, it would be unwise—even dangerous—to ignore him. "Everywhere it was recognized that 'git' and 'you git,' if unheeded, were possible curtain-raisers to bullets," writes one historian. "Mules might safely disregard 'giddap' or 'glang,' but they knew that 'you mules, git' prophesied the hissing of the whip lash."[31]

Even though cowboys prided themselves on their colorful language, they had no use for fancy multisyllabic words. Such talk was boastful and pretentious, they felt, and deserved to be mocked. If a man tried out a big word in conversation, say historians, other cowboys would often take out their pistols and pretend to shoot at the word, as if it were a pest. After a fancy word slipped out of the poor cowboy's mouth, writes one historian, "Another might shout, 'Where'd it go—there it is!' and blaze away at a dark corner where the ornery critter was hiding."[32]

"The Salt and Pepper of Ordinary Speech"

Swearing was perhaps the most obvious sign of cowboy speech. "Cowboy talk assayed somewhere around one-third profanity and obscenity," suggests one authority, "which was either directed at horses and cattle or

In this Remington painting titled The Quarrel *one cowboy challenges another. Such quarrels were not uncommon among men who were forced to live in close company for months at a time.*

Cowboys sit around the chuckwagon at mealtime. The expressions on their faces reveal why they were often deemed "humorless" by outsiders.

used as the salt and pepper of ordinary speech."[33] It is important to note that while strings of obscenities might sometimes signal anger or frustration on the part of the cowboy, such words were usually used simply for emphasis.

The phrase "son of a bitch" was used in almost every sentence uttered on the range, say some historians, and was even the name of a common stew eaten on the range. The word "damn" was used before nearly every noun. "Damn" also was used to mean "very" or "nearly." As cowboy authority Philip Ashton Rollins notes, "Thus, 'promptly at one o'clock' and 'immediately' might . . . come from a puncher's lips as 'at damned one' and 'damned now.'"[34]

Cowboys also had special, private swear words. Friends knew that if they heard a man's personal profanity, he was at his most angry.

One historian recalls three cowboys, Snake, Pinto Bill, and Nebrasky, who had such private words. No one, he writes, became too excited when they heard the regular "damns" and other oaths. "But, when Snake said icily, 'My own Aunt Mary!' or Pinto fairly hissed, 'My dead sister's doll!' or Nebrasky quietly but firmly remarked, 'Little Willie's goat!' some individual either ducked or 'dug for his cannon,' or else a horse or steer learned how it felt to be martyred."[35]

The Fun-Loving Cowboy

One visitor to the West remarked in 1886 that the cowboys, while interesting to talk with, were not particularly fun-loving. They seemed to him humorless and thin-skinned—lacking the ability to take a joke:

The Death of the Hat

In his book The Chisholm Trail: High Road of the Cattle Kingdom, *Don Worcester explains the kind of humor used by cowboys to test newcomers. If someone could take a joke, says Worcester, he was considered acceptable to everyone—as seen in the way cowboys treated a gentleman from the East who wore a large silk hat.*

"He [the gentleman from the East] lay down for a nap under an oak tree, placing the hat on the ground by his side. He was awakened by the tramp of horses' hoofs as the cowboys rode into camp, and he listened to their talk.

'What must we do?' one asked.

'What is it?'

'It's a bear.'

'It's a venomous kypote. It's one of those things that flew up and down the creek and hollowed wala wahoo in the night time.'

'Boys,' one cowboy said, 'it's a shame to stand peaceably by and see a good man devoured by that varmint.' He called, 'Look out there, mister, that thing will bite you,' and drew his pistol. The old gentleman 'got a ten cent move on him' and didn't stop to get his hat. By the time he was ten or fifteen feet away, every man had put a bullet or two through the hat, shooting the crown off.

Finally, one of the cowboys dismounted and, with a stick, cautiously turned the hat over. 'Boys, it's shore dead,' he said. The old gentleman had a hearty laugh, called the cowboys to his wagon, and took out a jug of 'sixteen-shooting liquor.' Together they celebrated the death of the terrible varmint. One of the cowboys lent him a hat until they could chip in and buy him one, the best to be had. After three days on his new ranch, everyone, including the cook, was ready to fight his battles for him."

I never saw elsewhere in this country a set of men that were so careful in the avoidance of sarcasm and smart sayings likely to give offense. They are severely matter-of-fact in everything, and very little given to joking. Indeed, where every man carries a six-shooter, jokes are not safe things to handle, unless they are of mighty small calibre.[36]

But other authorities on the Old West disagree. They say that although cowboys usually were reluctant to show a sense of humor to strangers, they did enjoy a good laugh. For example, they loved to sneak up and rope one another from behind bushes. A cowboy who snored could be "taught a lesson" by having his beard coated with pie dough as he slept. And goading another man's horse when he was lighting a cigarette or catching a catnap in the saddle was a source of great amusement, especially when the butt of the joke tumbled off his startled horse.

Discomfort and pain—of another man, of course—were particularly amusing to cowboys. A man might have something sharp or gooey slipped into his boots while he was asleep. And one historian writes that the funniest sight in the world to a veteran cowhand was "a greenhorn who had suffered a sprained ankle or dislocated shoulder from falling off his horse."[37]

Humor often helped cowboys laugh about subjects that frightened them—especially death. One historian reports that a man known as Lame Johnny, "whose only claim to immortality was a mouth big enough to plop a cantaloupe into," had been shot while trying to steal a horse. One of his killers felt that even a horse thief should have an epitaph, and finally came up with the following:

"Lame Johnny"
Stranger, pass gently over this sod.
If he opens his mouth, you're gone,
by God![38]

Practical jokes were used as a weapon against those who were not working as hard as the rest. One cowboy recalls a big man named Tall Cotton who had a habit of finding a place to nap during duty hours, leaving the other cowboys to do his share of the work. One day the men discovered Cotton asleep in a haystack, his boots off. They found a huge tarantula, killed it, and set it next to Cotton's leg. Then they jabbed the sleeping man a couple of times with a pin tied on the end of a long stick.

According to the story, as Cotton awoke screaming, dancing around in pain and fright, one cowboy rushed up and ground the tarantula under the heel of his boot. Writes one witness:

Cotton took one look at the dead tarantula and turned white. He began to get sick, even though the other [men] did their best to console him with stories of the horrible deaths they had seen as a result of tarantula bites. Finally, one of the crew, who laid claim to having read *Ten Thousand Things Worth Knowing,*

as well as *Dr. Chase's Recipe Book,* offered to try to save Cotton, even though he admitted it seemed hopeless.

First the cowboy poured a pint of bear's oil down Cotton. When that started the poison coming out of him, they followed it up with a glass of soda, a cup of vinegar, and finally a quart of water in which a plug of tobacco had been soaking. For a while it seemed almost certain that Cotton was going to die from that terrible tarantula bite; but the medicine was potent and, eventually, he was saved. After that, the crew had very little trouble with him lying down on the job, especially in haystacks.[39]

"Greasers" and "Niggers"

Although humor helped ease tense situations and enabled people to share laughs, there was one subject humor did not touch—racism. Although in the late nineteenth century no cowboy would have understood the word, the concept was not unknown. According to one historian, "cowboys were unabashed racists. Blacks were casually referred to as 'niggers.' Mexicans were 'greasers.'"[40]

Although many Mexican cowboys possessed skills that were envied by North American cowboys, they were thought of as lazy, as drunks, and as people who could not be trusted. During his days on the ranch, Theodore Roosevelt observed:

Some of the cowboys are Mexicans, who generally do the actual work well enough, but are not trustworthy; moreover, they are always regarded with extreme disfavor by the Texans in an outfit, among whom the intolerant caste spirit is very strong. Southern-born whites will never work under them, and look down upon all colored or half-caste races.[41]

If Mexican cowboys presented a problem for Anglos, the presence of large numbers of black cowboys was even more troublesome. For many white cowboys, natives of states in which slavery was a part of life, the idea of racial equality was unthinkable. And although the Civil War had resulted in the end of slavery in the South, few cowboys seemed willing to respect the new laws guaranteeing equal rights for all.

Although black cowboys were hired by white ranchers, they were almost always denied promotion to safer, better-paying positions. They were not allowed to become trail bosses, to acquire a herd of their own, or to buy a ranch. One black cowboy named Jim Perry worked twenty years at the huge XIT Ranch in Texas without getting promoted. There were seven large divisions in the ranch, and plenty of opportunities for white cowboys. "If it weren't for my damned old black face," Perry remarked, "I'd have been boss of one of these divisions long ago."[42]

Even So, Better than Most

But there are many historians who claim that even though the cattle industry in the late nineteenth century was run by former rebels of the Confederacy, it was considerably better than other businesses of the time. Black men who had cowboy skills could get jobs—although admittedly the work was more difficult and less likely to result in promotion. In the years following

Although they still confronted prejudice, Mexican and black cowboys were judged by their skills on the range.

the Civil War, however, few employment possibilities of any description existed for black Americans.

Historian Kenneth Wiggins Porter writes that black cowboys in Texas "frequently enjoyed greater opportunities for a dignified life than anywhere else in the United States. They worked, ate, slept, played, and on occasion fought, side by side with their white comrades, and their ability and courage won respect, even admiration."[43]

A black cowboy usually received the same wages as a white cowboy, and despite problems in the Old West, the difficulty of the job and the dangers involved often drew men together—even though words like "nigger" and "greaser" were used without apology. Porter continues:

The cow country was no utopia, but it demonstrates that under some circumstances and for at least brief periods whites and blacks in significant numbers could live and work together on more nearly equal terms than had been possible in the United States for 200 years or would be possible again for nearly another century.[44]

As much as his personality, a cowboy's manner of dress distinguished him from men engaged in other occupations. At first, many cowboys wore the remnants of their army attire—a raggedy gray Confederate uniform jacket or a pair of navy blue wool Union pants with a yellow stripe on their sides. As soon as they had a few dollars, however, cowboys invested in clothes that were more suitable for the job.

The "uniform" of a cowboy was, of course, designed to be practical. The work and the weather could be brutally hard on clothing, so what cowboys wore had to be rugged and well made. Not only that, but since cowboys had nowhere to store seasonal wardrobes while riding the range, their clothes had to be appropriate for both cold and hot weather.

The Fashionable Cowboy

Although durability and practicality were the basis of the cowboy's wardrobe, fashion played its part, too. Every cowboy seemed to be able to place his personal stamp on his clothing. "Cowboys were singularly appearance-conscious," writes one historian, "sometimes real dandies in their own steel-and-leather fashion."[45] Charles M. Russell, who was famous for his paintings of the Old West, agreed. He wrote that cowboys

> were mighty particular about their rig, an' in all the camps you'd find a fashion

Charles Russell dressed in full regalia. A cowboy had to wear well-made clothes that could take a beating.

> leader. From a cowpuncher's idea, these fellers was sure good to look at, an' I tell you right now, there ain't no prettier sight for my eyes than one of those good-lookin', long-backed cowpunchers,

"A Person of Thrill and Consequence"

In his book Cowboy Life: Reconstructing an American Myth, *William W. Savage Jr. quotes author Alfred Henry Lewis, who wrote about the American cowboy. Lewis describes the "cowboy look," which seemed to matter greatly to many men who rode the open range.*

"Your cowboy at that time [of the open range] was a person of thrill and consequence. He wore a broad-brimmed Stetson hat, and all about it a rattlesnake skin by way of band, retaining head and rattles. This was to be potent against headaches—a malady, by the way, which swept down no cowboy save in hours emergent of a spree. In such case the snake cure didn't cure. The hat was retained in defiance of winds, by a leathern cord caught about the back of the head, not under the chin. This cord was beautiful with a garniture of three or four perforated poker chips, red, yellow, and blue.

There are sundry angles of costume where the dandyism of a cowboy of spirit and conceit may acquit itself; these are hatband, spurs, saddle, and leggins. I've seen hatbands made of braided gold and silver filigree; they were from Santa Fe, and always in the form of a rattlesnake, with rubies or emeralds or diamonds for eyes. Such gauds would cost from four hundred to two thousand dollars. Also, I've encountered a saddle which depleted its proud owner a round twenty-five hundred dollars. It was of finest Spanish leather, stamped and spattered with gold bosses. There was gold-capping on the saddle horn, and again on the circle of the cantle. . . . Your cowboy dandy frequently wears wrought steel spurs, inlaid with silver and gold; price, anything you please. If he flourish a true [dandy] of the plains his leggins will be gronted from instep to belt with the thick pelt, hair outside, of a Newfoundland dog. The hair of the Newfoundland, thick and long and laid the right way, defies the rains, and your cowboy loathes water."

sittin' up on a . . . saddle with a live hoss between his legs.[46]

The foundation of the cowboy's costume was hidden—a pair of red or gray wool long johns, worn in cold and hot weather alike. The underwear not only kept a cowboy warm in winter but, in the heat of the summer, absorbed sweat that would otherwise rot shirts and pants. The long johns had a "convenience flap" in the back, so that when relieving himself a cowboy didn't have to take off more clothes than necessary!

Over his long underwear, the cowboy wore a collarless shirt of heavy cotton or wool. The shirt might be a plaid or print, or a solid color. The only color shirt cowboys did not wear was red, for as one historian noted, that color "was reputed to go badly among the cattle, and, in any event, belonged to the miners."[47]

On top of the shirt went a vest—never buttoned, for most cowboys believed that to button up would cause them to catch cold. Sometimes the vest was a striped, woven Mexican waistcoat, other times a woolen or canvas fabric. The vest was important, for it gave the cowboy another layer of protection from the wind and weather. But its most useful aspect was its many deep pockets. Since pants pockets were virtually useless to a man sitting all day on a horse, it was necessary to put small personal items in vest pockets.

What sort of personal items did cowboys need on the range? The vast majority were

The cowboy's outfit usually included a vest. The vest's pockets held the cowboy's necessities, including his cigarettes.

smokers, so matches, cigarette papers, and a stash of Bull Durham tobacco were carried in the vest. (Interestingly, since matches of the day were sold loose, there was no matchbook cover on which to strike them, and the cowboy used the seat of his pants for that job. He would first lift his knee to tighten the fabric across his pants seat, and then draw a brown-tipped match quickly across.)

There were some less-than-practical things carried in the vest's deep pockets, too. Many cowboys were collectors—anything that looked unusual or interesting was picked up and saved for a later day, to show off to friends, or to be kept for luck. Arrowheads, gold nuggets, and especially elk or buffalo teeth were saved in this way. Historians say that while the teeth were saved with the idea of trading them, cowboys also acquired them "because of a vague, boy-like idea that somehow, someday, they might be useful. In reality, as [the cowboy] got them, he gave them to Eastern souvenir hunters, as he also gave the nuggets and the arrowheads."[48]

Keeping His Pants Up

Most cowboys in the immediate postwar period wore woolen pants. Belts weren't worn, except for a rare social occasion, for a cowboy wearing a belt buckle on a bucking horse risked serious injury. And many cowboys complained that suspenders chafed their skin and caused sores. Therefore, pants were worn tight in the waist, to keep them up.

Some cowboys, borrowing an item from the *vaquero*'s wardrobe, used a green or red silk sash as a belt. The sashes were considered lucky, and very fashionable as they flapped in the breeze as the cowboy raced along on his horse. One old-time cowboy named Charles

A 1910 advertisement for Levis uses cowboys to boast of the ruggedness of the jeans. Cowboys seemed the ultimate test of the pants' durability.

The Flag of Cattle Country

No cowboy would consider riding the range without a bright red bandanna knotted loosely around his neck. This piece of cloth was unofficially known as the flag of cattle range country, for it was useful in so many ways.

The most common use was as a mask to keep dust out of a man's nose and throat. Cowboys on the plains, especially the "tail riders" who rode behind the herd, where dust was kicked up in clouds, wore their bandannas up to their eyes. But a dust mask was only the most obvious of the bandanna's uses. Historian Dee Brown chronicled the ways the bandanna was used:

> To protect the back of the neck from the sun; an ear cover in cold weather; a towel; a blindfold for skittery horses; for tying a calf's legs together when branding it; as a strainer for drinking muddy water; a dish drier; a hat tie in windy weather; a sling for broken arms; a bandage; as an aid in hand signaling; a face covering for dead cowboys; for hanging horse thieves.[50]

Although bandannas were manufactured in red, white, blue, green, yellow, and brown, most cowboys believed red was a lucky color. And while only red bandannas were worn at work, most men kept a spare of another color for dances or other rare social events.

Soft Hands and Embroidered Gauntlets

Most cowboys wore gloves. They might be made of the finest buckskin, leather, or horsehide. Whatever the material, the gloves had to be made well so that they didn't stiffen and become hard and uncomfortable when

Siringo continued to wear his red sash long after his trail-riding days were over. "Finally my silk sash disappeared," Siringo later wrote, "and another couldn't be purchased in this northern country. There was nothing to do but wear suspenders to keep my pants up, which almost broke my heart."[49]

By the 1880s a new kind of pants was very popular among ranch workers. Invented by Levi Strauss, these pants were blue or brown denim, with copper rivets reinforcing the pockets. Strauss's new pants had been invented with California's gold miners in mind, for the rivets kept the pockets from tearing when they were jammed full of gold nuggets and rock samples. The durability of the pants—known later as Levis—made them useful to cowboys, too.

they got wet. They were helpful in cold weather for warmth, of course. However, their most important function was to protect the hands from blisters and burns from both reins and lariat. Although, as one historian writes, "some scorned gloves of any kind, claiming they robbed a man of a good feel on the rope," for many cowboys gloves were a welcome protection.[51]

A large number of cowboys wore their gloves constantly—every waking hour—for they felt that gloved hands were a status symbol. A cowboy who never removed his gloves was showing the world that "his riding and roping was so excellent as to excuse him from all other tasks." The same author adds that "the hands of such men frequently were as white and soft as those of a young girl."[52]

Cowboy gloves were usually yellow, or a greenish, creamy white. Quite often cowboys wore leather gauntlets, or cuffs, that came five or six inches past their wrists. These gauntlets, of course, gave added protection to the wrists and arms—however, fashion certainly played a role. Most gauntlets were decorated, embroidered with silk thread, or with thin silver or brass wire, and there was often fringe sewn on the little-finger side of each. Sometimes the pattern of the decoration was geometric, although Texas stars or spread eagles were common images on cowboy gauntlets.

Little Feet and Mule Ears

One of the most important parts of the American cowboy's wardrobe was his boots. Indeed, leather boots set him apart from ordinary, earthbound men. "He is proud that he is a horseman," writes one observer, "and he has contempt for all human beings who walk. . . . On foot in his tight, stumpy, tight-toed boots he is lost. But he wishes you to understand that he is never on foot."[53]

Small feet were greatly esteemed by cowboys, and tight-fitting boots accentuated this trait. Farmers, miners, and other workers wore boots, too, but unlike the cowboy's boots, they were heavy and clumsy looking. The man on the range, said one cowboy, could be identified easily because he "put his feet into decent boots, and not into entire cows."[54]

So important was it to have small feet, in fact, that many cowboys would squeeze into boots a size or two too small just to get the desired effect. As one writer states, "no

A cowboy wears two common wardrobe components—gloves and a bandanna. Some cowboys wore their gloves constantly as a kind of status symbol.

An Indispensable Tool

In his book The Cowboys, *author William Forbis explains some of the many uses cowboys had for a rope, or lariat. As Forbis shows, the reasons for a rope's value run a wide spectrum from useful to violent.*

"Expertly thrown, a rope could snare a cow's horns or a horse's neck, or the hooves of either, enabling a 140-pound man to capture and subdue a 1,000-pound animal. A rope could be transformed into an instant corral when it was stretched taut by several men. It could be used as a hobble to keep a horse from straying away in the night. Hitched around a saddle horn, it served to drag firewood or pull a mired cow out of a bog. And although violence was far less common in the West than the legends have it, the rope was on certain rare occasions shaped into a hangman's noose to carry out short-order justice, served up quick and hot when someone was caught in an absolutely unforgivable crime such as horse stealing. Cowboys even dreamed up some magical functions for rope; they believed, for example, that if one made

The rope was an essential tool and had a variety of uses. A cowboy's level of expertise with a rope also lent him status among his peers.

of horsehair was placed in a circle around a sleeping man, it would protect him from snakes."

amount of discomfort was held to justify surrendering the illusion."[55] New boots were soaked in water and worn nonstop for several days (and nights) so that they could fit a man's feet like a second layer of skin.

The boots varied in design and decoration, but they were alike in many important respects. They were at least seventeen inches tall, protecting the cowboy's feet and lower legs from brush, thorns, and sharp cattle horns. They had a high, underslung heel, so a cowboy's feet would stay in the stirrups more securely. And because the leading cause of death for cowboys was being dragged by a horse, boots had sharp, pointy toes—good for getting feet in and out of stirrups fast.

Because of the emphasis on a tight fit, boots were equipped with straps to help the cowboy pull them on. The straps were known as "mule ears," for they were shaped exactly like the real thing. As one historian reports, the best way to pull on a tight cowboy boot is "standing, stepping down into it, and hauling firmly on the . . . mule ears, while trying to avoid hopping around and cursing!"[56]

An old cowboy named Teddy Blue Abbott recalls with great fondness how he had spent his whole paycheck from his first trail drive on clothes. The purchase of which he was most proud was a pair of custom-made boots,

A boot from 1900 shows the features a cowboy considered essential—straps for pulling the tight-fitting boot on, and the heel, which was specially made to hug the stirrup.

which he wore according to the latest fashion—pant legs tucked inside. According to Abbott, however, the look did not have the desired effect on his family:

I remember like it was yesterday. I had a new white Stetson hat that I paid ten dollars for and new pants that cost twelve dollars, and a good shirt and fancy boots. They had colored tops, red and blue, with a half-moon and star on them. Lord, I was proud of those clothes. . . . I believe one reason I went home was just so I could show them off. But when I got there and my sister saw me, she said, "Take your pants out of your boots and put your coat on. You look like an outlaw."

[Says Abbott] I told her to go to hell. . . . And I never did like her after that.[57]

A Hat for All Seasons

There was no more personal item of clothing in the cowboy's wardrobe than his hat. Referred to as a "conk cover," "lid," "war bonnet," or "hair case," the cowboy's hat was modeled after the *vaquero*'s sombrero. Its brim was wide and the crown was sometimes eight inches tall. A good cowboy hat provided enough shade to protect the wearer's head, face, and shoulders as well.

Like the bandanna, the cowboy's hat had many uses. Not only was it a head covering, it was a good means of signaling to another cowboy. One historian specified that

in rainy weather it served as an umbrella. The brim, when grasped between the thumb and fingers and bent into a trough, was on its upper surface the only drinking

Only One Hat

One brand of hat was most popular on the prairies and ranches of the Old West—the Stetson. Named after its designer, John B. Stetson, the hat could be used in a number of different ways, according to Lewis Nordyke, quoted in Lon Tinkle's and Allen Maxwell's anthology, The Cowboy Reader.

"In case of emergency the cowboy carried oats or corn in the crown for his horse; many a cowboy climbed into almost inaccessible places, dipped up water in his hat, and carried it out to his horse; or cupped the brim and used it as his own drinking vessel. A prospector caught in the desert with a leaky canteen conserved his water by pouring it in his Stetson; a ranger caught in a forest fire buried himself in the ground, leaving only his face exposed. He covered his face with his Stetson; when rescuers found him, he was uninjured, but his hat was badly charred.

The Stetson was handy for fanning campfires into life, for blindfolding or whipping stubborn horses, for slapping ornery steers in the face, for fighting grass fires, for replacing broken window panes, for dummy or actual targets in gun fights. Then the cowboy brushed it with his elbow and wore it to town or to the Saturday night dance. A Stetson with a bullet hole in it has always been a prize possession with Westerners, and there's a common expression: 'You can put a dozen bullet holes in a Stetson

the last drop from his STETSON

A 1920s advertisement for Stetson hats capitalizes on just one of many uses the hat provided the cowboy.

and it won't ravel.' When you own a big Stetson you don't brag about how new it is but about how old it is. Many a Stetson has been in service twenty to thirty years, and a hat that old is a prized family heirloom. A Stetson will take on weight and it will get to the point where you can smell it across the room, but you can't wear it out."

cup of the outdoors; when pulled down and tied over the ears, it gave complete protection from frostbite. It fanned into activity every campfire started in the open, and enlarged the carrying capacity of the hat when used as a pail to transport water for extinguishing embers.[58]

A Philadelphian, J.B. Stetson, made more cowboy hats than any other hatmaker, and so the words "Stetson" and "hat" became interchangeable on the range. Stetsons were made of high-quality felt—usually dove gray, tan, or black.

A Personal Statement

Around the crown of the hat, just above the brim, ran a band. Many cowboys liked a leather band, but Texas cowboys seemed to prefer thin braided wire of gold or silver. The band was almost always a way for a cowboy to personalize his hat.

Leather bands were often studded with ornamental nails; wire bands had flat plates of silver or gold woven onto them. Many cowboys strung "treasures" onto their hatbands, such as a skull of a snake or small desert animal, a rattle from a rattlesnake, or an interesting arrowhead. Some cowboys created their own bands, using a rattlesnake skin, or a rein from a favorite horse.

How a hat was worn was a sure indicator of where a cowboy came from. Texans and other southwesterners liked the crown of the hat high, whereas cowboys from northern states usually crushed the top down in a series of creases. A cowboy who wanted to pretend he was from Texas could do so by punching out the creases in his hat!

However it was worn, the hat was the most noticeable trademark of the American cowboy. Historians say that many cowboys felt incomplete without a hat, even at bedtime. Proof of cowboys' reluctance to remove their hats was easy to find—every cowboy had a bone white forehead. In fact, in Indian sign language, the symbol for a white man was made by passing the fingers across the forehead.

"When He Did, He Needed It Like Hell"

The gun was a big part of the mythology of the American cowboy, and was the one bit of equipment most associated with him. Interestingly, however, the popular image of the cowboy with a six-shooter on each hip is inaccurate. Cowboy Teddy Blue Abbott wrote:

> There is one thing I would like to get straight. I punched cows from '71 [1871] on, and I never saw a cowboy with two guns, I mean two six-shooters. Wild Bill [Hickock] carried two guns and so did some of those other city marshals, like Bat Masterson, but they were professional gunmen themselves, not cowpunchers. But a cowboy with two guns is all movie stuff, and so is this business of a gun on each hip.[59]

Cowboys *did* carry guns, but one would have to look carefully to spot them. Rifles were hard to carry on horseback, for the scabbard used to hold them rubbed against the horse's hide and caused welts. Wearing a belted holster for a pistol was uncomfortable for a man in the saddle all day. Some cowboys stored a gun in their bedroll, or more often, in a box in the supply wagon while on the trail.

Although, as Teddy Blue Abbott stressed, most cowboys were not sharpshooters with

Although cowboys did not need their guns often, choosing to carry them in their bedrolls or even in the supply wagon, the weapon was an essential part of life on the range.

guns ready at every moment, it was still true that the Old West could be a very dangerous place. According to an old Texas saying, the cowboy "didn't need [a gun] often, but when he did, he needed it like hell."[60]

There were surprise visits by rattlesnakes, occasional Indian raids, and brushes with criminals intent on stealing the cattle or horses in a cowboy's care. Sometimes a crazed steer or wounded horse had to be put out of its misery. Cowboys also used their guns to shoot any lone dogs they spotted. The animals may not have been dangerous, but dogs were known to go after calves occasionally, and the cowboy could take no chances. As one historian writes, "every strange and unattended canine found wandering on the range was prejudged to have a murderous intent, and was sentenced and executed on sight."[61]

One of the most common uses, however, was simply show. Most cowboys would never consider calling on a woman without a gun, for the six-shooter was part of his masculine image. As one historian writes, "The gun not only was an integral part of full dress, but also was to the mind of the cowboy as effective on the female heart, and as compelling an accompaniment of lovemaking as to the belief of the young soldier has ever been the sword."[62]

"Sam Colt Made Them All Equal"

The weapon of choice was the Colt .45, the gun known as the six-shooter—so called because unlike earlier guns, which had to be reloaded after each round, it held six bullets. Named after its inventor, Samuel Colt, the Colt .45 was hailed as an "equalizer"—a weapon that everyone could use for protection from outlaws and other dangers. "God made some men big and some men small," one old saying went, "but Sam Colt made them all equal."[63]

The revolver weighed between two and four pounds. The first six-shooters were quite

All a Cowboy Needs . . . **43**

bulky, with a barrel a foot long. By the end of the Civil War, the barrels had been cut to six or seven inches. The gun could be purchased at general stores and trading posts, as well as through mail-order catalogs. The handle was black rubber, pearl, or ivory, depending on what a cowboy could afford and how much status he wanted.

A Dangerous Toy

Besides impressing women and protecting their owners from danger, cowboys' guns were toys—useful diversions from boredom. Relaxing in the bunkhouse when work was slow, cowboys enjoyed engaging in good-natured target practice. Sometimes they shot at a picture calendar or sign on the wall, and sometimes, as one cowboy remembers, more lively targets.

> I stopped for supper at the Circle I ranch. While waiting for dinner I lay on my back in the bunk room and counted 362 bullet holes in the ceiling. They came to be there because the festive cowboys used to while away the time lying as I was lying while waiting for supper in shooting the flies that crawled about the plaster.[64]

But for all the stories of lighthearted gunplay, there are many instances of guns misfiring, or going off unintentionally, and causing injuries. Many cowboys, having inflicted injuries on themselves, lied about their wounds, telling others that the scars were caused by more heroic circumstances. One cowboy recalls a man named Billy who led his friends to believe he'd been hurt in a

An advertisement for the Colt six-shooter pictures the cowboy, who chose the weapon because it was readily available and held six bullets.

gunfight, although in fact he'd acquired his wounds as he went to wash up one morning:

> There was a bench standing just outside the hut, and in his hurry, and half asleep, he stumbled over it, and as he fell his six-shooter jerked loose out of his hip pocket and went off, [the bullet] passing through Billy's cheek and grazing the bone. . . . That was how Billy got his bullet wound in the cheek; not in a gunfight.[65]

From Brushpopping to Roundups

A s the Texas ranchers returned after the Civil War, they soon realized that getting the stock to market was not the only obstacle they faced. In their absence, there had been some worrisome changes in the cattle themselves.

The herds had scattered; many had wandered far from the ranches. In addition, the Confederate army had taken many cattle to feed the troops—without compensating the ranchers. Other cattle had been taken in Indian raids. Meanwhile, calves had been born, grown to maturity, and given birth themselves during the four years the ranchers had

Texas longhorn steers were particularly fierce. In order to brand the semi-wild longhorns, cowboys had to lure them out of the brush.

been away. None of these cattle were branded, of course, so there was considerable confusion as to who owned which animals. In addition, many bulls had reverted to the "wild" pattern of savagely fighting for females. (Normally, ranchers castrated most bulls, to prevent such aggressive behavior.)

Before they could be driven north to the railroad line in Kansas and sold, therefore, the cattle had to be gathered and sorted out for branding. Roundups have never been easy, but the first ones after the Civil War were particularly difficult, for the cattle had become wilder and more unmanageable than ever. As one historian later remarked, the cows had "gleefully led a life of saucy independence."[66]

Wild Cattle

Most of the cattle born after the ranchers had left for the war had never seen a human. Likewise, to the young men arriving in Texas to become cowboys—especially to those from the North and East who were not familiar with Texas cattle—the "cows" must have been a shocking sight. While many of the range cattle were a mixture of short-horned eastern cattle and the Spanish longhorns, there were still a large number of the fierce, pure-bred longhorns roaming the prairies.

"Tall, bony, coarse-headed and coarse-haired, flat-sided, thin-flanked, swaybacked, big-eared, with tails dragging the ground and legs that belonged to a race horse, they lumbered through the [brush] and over the plain, grotesque to the critical eye and beautiful to the sentimentalist cowboy," according to historians Joe B. Frantz and Julian Ernest Choate Jr.[67] The horns were amazing, measuring between three and five feet from tip to tip—some spanning nine feet!

The longhorns were not only big, they were powerful. One witness testified that "with their steel hoofs, their long legs, their staglike muscles, their thick skins, their powerful horns, they could walk the roughest ground, cross the widest deserts, climb the highest mountains, swim the widest rivers,

The Brush Horse

The work known as "brushpopping" was difficult not only for the cowboys, but for their horses as well. Famous cowboy authority J. Frank Dobie writes about the brush horse in his book A Vaquero of the Brush Country, *quoted in* The Cowboy Reader, *edited by Lon Tinkle and Allen Maxwell.*

"Let us draw a picture. Down in a *ramadero* of spined bushes and trees that seem to cover all space except that occupied by prickly pear, a man with scratched face, frazzled ducking jacket, and snagged leggins is sitting on a horse, one leg thrown over the horn of his saddle. He is humped forward and seems to be almost asleep. The horse has grey hairs in his flanks; his knees are lumped from licks and thorns of past years. He is an old-timer and knows the game. He is resting one hip and he seems to be asleep. The man is waiting, for some other *vaqueros* have entered the *ramadero* above him to start up the wild cattle. Presently he thinks that he catches the high note of a yell far up the brush; he feels a quiver in the muscles of his horse. The horse thinks that he hears too; he no longer appears to be asleep; his ears are cocked. A minute later the sound of the yell is unmistakable.

The brush hand takes down his leg; the horse plants down the leg he has been resting and holds his head high, ears working. Again the yell, closer.

Pretty soon the popping of brush made by the running cattle will be heard. There will not be many cattle in the bunch, however—just three or four or a half-dozen. Outlaws like company but they are not gregarious. The *vaquero's* feet are planted deep in the stirrups now. *Pop—scratch*—silence. In what direction was that sound? The old horse's heart is beating like a drum against the legs of his rider. *Pop—scr-r-ratch*—rattle and rake of hoofs. Man and horse hit the brush as one. They understand each other. They may get snagged, knocked by limbs that will not break, cut, speared, pierced with black thorns, the poison from which sends cold chills down the back of the man and makes him sick at the stomach. No matter. The horse and rider go like a pair of mated dogs charging a boar. The brush tears and pops as if a pair of Missouri mules were running through it with a mowing machine. Hell pops. The brush hand is in his element."

fight off the fiercest band of wolves, endure hunger, cold, thirst, and punishment as few beasts of the earth have ever shown themselves capable of enduring."[68]

Far wilder than the other cattle, the longhorns remained hidden in the thick brush and cactus of the Texas landscape. They stayed out of sight during the daylight hours, emerging from their hiding places at night to graze. Writes one cowboy:

They was even harder to get a sight of than any wild deer. They'd always see you first and had the sage chicken beat when it came to hiding; they'd stand still as a petrified tree and let you ride past within a few yards of 'em if they thought they was well enough hid. But if there was no hiding place handy they'd take to running, and I never yet seen a horse that could catch up with 'em in their brushy, rocky territory.[69]

Mossy Horns

The most dangerous of the wild cattle, called "mossy horns" by the cowboys, were steers ten to twelve years old—the herd leaders. To the returning Texas ranchers, they were nothing but trouble. "These were outlaws when it came to being herded by men on horses," explains one Texas historian, "and it was necessary to clear them out as quickly as possible, for they made younger cattle more difficult to handle. Mossy horns were as wild as mustangs, and they preserved their freedom with determination."[70] The ranchers were anxious to capture these mossy horns first, and sell them before they could turn an entire herd into an unruly, fierce mob.

Mossy horns lived everywhere on the wide-open prairies of the West, but they were able to stay wild longer in the Southwest, particularly in a part of Texas called the Brasada, between the Nueces River and the Rio Grande. The terrain was filled with cactus plants, thickets, and underbrush, which provided the animals with lots of hiding places.

The problem of capturing the mossy horns and removing them from the range was one of the most difficult a cowboy had to face. The process was known as "brushpopping," and it was the most dangerous kind of cow work. The cowboys—or "brushpoppers," as these specialized workers were called—relied heavily on mustangs or cow ponies. Descended from the horses brought

Breaking wild horses to the saddle was another task for the cowboy.

to the New World by the Spanish explorers, the mustangs were small, quick, and smart, and seemed to enjoy chasing the lightning-fast steers.

There was almost an endless supply of mustangs, for like cattle, they ran wild on the range. Unfortunately, this made the little horses expendable, at least in the eyes of the cowboys. The mustangs were ridden hard and into dangerous situations. They were often gored to death by the angry steers, or crippled before their work was done.

Brushpopping

In the early days of cattle ranching, cowboys used several systems to rid the ranges of mossy horns. The most common was to try to lure them out of hiding by means of a "decoy herd"—a group of cattle a little tamer than most, that wouldn't bolt at the sight of a man on horseback.

Before releasing the decoy herd, brush-poppers built a makeshift corral near where they believed wild cattle might be hiding. One cowboy described the process: "A trench some three feet deep was dug in the ground. Strong posts about ten feet long were then placed on end, closely together in these trenches, and the ground tramped firmly about them. They were then lashed together about five feet above the ground with long strips of green cowhide."[71]

This corral would be the holding pen for any wild cattle caught. As soon as a mossy horn was spotted, the cowboys led the decoys close by and surrounded the area. If the plan worked, the mossy horns charged out of their hiding places, toward the decoys. Usually the horses sensed the approach of the wild cattle first. What happened next was controlled more by the horses than their riders. One historian explains:

> When [the horses] heard cattle crashing through the brush, the eager ponies dashed after them, their riders hanging on and dodging tree limbs and prickly pears [cactus] as best they could. Some of the ponies threw themselves sideways through the thickets. A rider might be anywhere on his pony except in the saddle; he was paid to hang on, not to main-

Cowboys flush the dangerous longhorns from the brush during a roundup.

"Make Me a Cowboy Again for a Day"

Many cowboy songs were simple melodies, often without words. However, there were many songs cowboys sang that celebrated the life of the cowboy during roundups and trail drives, complete with the hardships and dangers of that life. In his book Cowboys of the Americas, *Richard Slatta quotes an old cowboy song entitled, "Make Me a Cowboy Again for a Day."*

Thunder of hoofs on the range as you ride,
Hissing of iron and sizzling of hide,
Bellows of cattle and snort of cayuse,
Longhorns from Texas as wild as the deuce.

Mid-nite stampedes and milling of herds,
Yells of the Cow-men too angry for words,
Right in the thick of it all would I say,
Make me a Cowboy again for a day.

Under the star-studded Canopy vast,
Camp-fire and coffee and comfort at last,
Bacon that sizzles and crisps in the pan,
After the roundup smells good to a man.
Stories of ranchers and rustler retold,
Over the Pipe as the embers grow cold,
Those are the times that old memories play,
Make me a Cowboy again for a day.

tain his dignity or look graceful, and brush ponies would not stop for anything once the chase began.[72]

Peculiar Melodies and Moonlit Nights

As the wild and tame grew into a unified herd, the cowboys surrounded them, keeping them together. And every description of brushpopping noted that the cowboys sang while they rode around the herd. One man mentioned "a peculiar melody without words,"[73] another described the cowboys' "loudly singing unmelodious tunes . . . presumably to calm the nervous cattle."[74] Whatever the intent, the songs must have been successful enough of the time to make them a key part of the process.

As the cowboys sang, they tried to ease the cattle out of the brush toward the corral.

If they were lucky, the decoys would have a slightly calming effect on the mossy horns, and a few of the "outlaws" would find their way into the corral. But for every time they were successful, at least once the brushpoppers would end up with fewer cattle in the corral than they had begun with—tame cows often were lured to a life in the brush with the mossy horns.

There were other ways, too, to capture mossy horns, but they were more dangerous. A brushpopper might go one-on-one with a steer, using his lariat to rope it. Hundreds of cowboys and ponies were injured or killed doing this, however, for a roped steer often charged the pony and rider. A quick-thinking cowboy facing a charging mossy horn was forced either to cut the rope and try to scramble for safety or to shoot the charging beast.

Another brushpopper trick was to wait for a moonlit night (for visibility) and start a

Chasing and roping a wild longhorn was one of the most dangerous jobs required of a cowboy. A roped longhorn could quickly turn and gore horse or rider.

stampede. Firing his six-shooter into the air, and whooping loudly, the cowboy charged into the brush, frightening the cattle. They ran mindlessly through the night, churning up the dust as they tried to escape the noise. Finally, after hours of running at top speed, the cattle stopped, too exhausted to fight the cowboy's efforts to control them.

Cruelty and Control

After wild cattle had been captured, they still had to be moved to a ranch, and later driven with a herd going to market. To accomplish this, the cattle had to be "settled"; and historians have pointed out that the process sometimes entailed cruelty.

A common form of settling a steer was to tie all four legs together. Not only did this make movement impossible, says one cowboy, but even after the animal was released, it was slowed down. According to brushpopper James Cook, "If [the steers] had been left for several hours, their legs would be so benumbed and stiffened that they could not run fast." Cook admits that while this method usually worked, occasionally steers were so anxious to get free that numb legs didn't stop them from making an escape. "Sometimes when regaining their feet they would charge at the nearest live object and keep right on through the bunch of cattle and line of riders. It would then be necessary to rope them . . . again."[75]

A particularly unruly mossy horn might be shot through the thickest part of its horn. The shock and excruciating pain would make the steer submissive. And, writes one expert, if the cowboy missed and killed the animal, it was no real loss. "Cowmen were determined to rid their ranges of troublesome mossy horns, and no one cared if a few were killed in the process."[76]

Probably the most inhumane way of settling a wild steer was to tie it securely to a tree or bush and cut its eyelids off. This mutilation did not kill the animal, but did discourage it from running back into the thick brush country. Writes cowboy Will James:

Them eyelids being took from 'em and leaving their eyes unprotected not only made 'em lose their liking for the thick brush, but it also took the fight out of 'em, for in both places them same eyelids are mighty necessary if the critter wants to keep her eyesight; a twig don't feel so good scraping along on a bare eye, and them critters knowed that without experimenting on it and kept out of trouble in that way. . . . They picked up on fat and gradually lost their wild ideas and speed.[77]

A Hard Life

Brushpoppers led a very difficult life, more dangerous and unpleasant than that of other cowboys. For one thing, the brush country was remote and lonely. For months at a time, men would live without mail, without contact from civilization. They were paid somewhat better than other cowhands, but there was nothing to spend money on in the Brasada.

Discomfort was part of the job. It usually took over an hour for a brushpopper to pick all the thorns from his clothing, his skin, and his pony at the end of a day. Even with pro-tective clothing, there was no way to avoid the millions of prickles from cacti, mesquite bushes, and other thorny plants.

Lice were a big problem for the brush-poppers, too. They were everywhere—on skin, in hair, in the bedrolls, and in every piece of clothing the men owned. The cowboys did learn a trick from the Native Americans that made their lives a bit easier—they put their clothes on ant hills each night, letting the ants carry off the lice. And when the lice became too thick in a man's hair, he washed it with a mixture of kerosene and coffee—and hoped for the best.

Besides being home to the wildest, most dangerous cattle, the brush country sheltered a host of outlaws—murderers, thieves, and other wanted men. In fact, the Nueces River was unofficially known as the "deadline

...tograph of **GEORGE PARKER.**   Description.

NAME, GEORGE PARKER, alias "BUTCH" CASSIDY, alias GEORGE CASSIDY, alias INGERFIELD.

AGE, 36 years (1901).	HEIGHT, 5 ft., 9 inches.
WEIGHT, 165 lbs.	BUILD, Medium.
COMPLEXION, light.	COLOR OF HAIR, flaxen.
EYES, blue.	MUSTACHE, sandy, if any.
NATIONALITY, American.	OCCUPATION, cowboy, rustler.

CRIMINAL OCCUPATION, bank robber and highwayman, cattle and horse thief.

MARKS, two cuts scars back of head, small scar under left eye, small brown mole calf of leg.

"BUTCH" CASSIDY is known as a criminal principally in Wyoming, Utah, Idaho, Colorado and Nevada and has served time in Wyoming State penitentiary at Laramie for grand larceny, but was pardoned January 19th, 1896.

...cription of **HARRY LONGBAUGH.**

..E, HARRY LONGBAUGH, alias "KID" LONGBAUGH, alias HARRY ALONZO.

35 to 40 years.	HEIGHT, 5 ft. 9 inches.	WEIGHT, 165 to 170 lbs.
..PLEXION, dark (looks like quarter breed Indian).	COLOR OF HAIR, black.	BUILD, rather slim.
..S, black.	MUSTACHE, if any, black.	NOSE, rather long.
..TURES, Grecian type.	NATIONALITY, American.	OCCUPATION, cowboy, rustler.

..INAL OCCUPATION, highwayman and bank burglar, cattle and horse thief.

..HARRY LONGBAUGH served 18 months in jail at Sundance, Cook Co., Wyoming, when a boy, for horse stealing. In ..ber, 1892, HARRY LONGBAUGH, Bill Madden and Harry Bass "held up" a Great Northern train at Malta, Mon-.. Bass and Madden were tried for this crime, convicted and sentenced to 10 and 14 years respectively; LONGBAUGH ..ed and since has been a fugitive. June 28, 1897, under the name of Frank Jones, Longbaugh participated with Harvey ..s, alias Curry, Tom Day and Walter Putney, in the Belle Fouche, S. D., bank robbery. All were arrested, but Longbaugh ..arvey Logan escaped from jail at Deadwood, October 31, 1897, and have not since been arrested.
..GEORGE PARKER, alias "BUTCH" CASSIDY, HARRY LONGBAUGH and a third man were implicated in the ..ry of the First National Bank of Winnemucca, Nevada, on September 19, 1900.

While hunting for stray cattle, a brushpopper might come across an outlaw like Butch Cassidy, hiding out from the law.

The chuckwagon was brought to a central location and loaded with supplies and food during roundups.

for sheriffs." With plenty of places to hide out, the criminals knew they were safe from the law. Brushpoppers adopted a "live and let live" attitude toward these outlaws, for it would have been foolish to tangle with criminals who were heavily armed and, in most cases, crackerjack shots. "Ranchers [in the Brasada] found it wiser to help fugitives than to arrest them," writes one historian, "for it was unhealthful to earn the enmity of men who lived outside the law."[78]

Most ranchers who employed brushpoppers treated them well, for they knew that cowboys good enough to capture wild steers were rare. Stories abounded of what happened when the job was left to amateurs. In one case, a herd of mossy horns was captured in the spring of 1872 and sold to a man from Kansas. He hired on inexperienced hands, and attempted to bring twelve hundred wild steers back to Kansas. Unfortunately, all the cattle escaped, en route, leaving the man with nothing. "Unaccustomed to handling

wild cattle," the account goes, "[the rancher and his hands] reached Kansas with only their saddle horses and work oxen. Some of the wild steers were back in the brush before the next year's cow hunt."[79]

More Methodical Roundups

Throughout the rest of Texas and the Southwest, mossy horns were not as much of a problem. There were longhorns, but many of these had bred with short-horned cattle and had become more used to humans. But although the cattle were not as vicious or wild, they still wandered far from their owners' ranches.

Ranchers hired cowboys called "line riders" to ride around the boundaries of their property, turning back cattle that had strayed too far from home. But these were the days before fences, and keeping thousands of cattle in a particular area was impossible. Many animals drifted two or three hundred miles from home.

Therefore, the spring roundup was a necessary part of ranch life. All the ranchers in a given area took part—some roundups in the late 1800s involved as many as twenty-five different ranchers in a five-thousand-square-mile area, and employed two or three hundred cowboys. Cattle had to be counted, however, and calves had to be branded. Every nearby rancher was motivated to participate by the knowledge of how far cattle strayed, and how quickly they multiplied in the mild Texas climate.

Getting Started

When a roundup was scheduled, the ranchers busied themselves with preparations. Horses had to be assembled, for cowboys did not use their own mounts for work—ranchers feared they might not ride their own horses hard enough. So several herds of cow ponies (six or seven for each cowboy) were brought to the central roundup site and corralled. A large chuckwagon, really a kitchen and supply closet on wheels, was stocked with food and other necessities and brought to the site.

A few days before the roundup began, cowboys began gathering from all directions. It was before the roundup that the fun took place—card games, music and singing, contests with lariats, and horse races. The most enjoyable part of the preroundup festivities was simply reuniting with other cowboys a man hadn't seen in a while. As one expert writes:

An old hand like Waddy Peacock could throw his arm around the shoulders of

Bread for the Cow Hunters

Many of the cow hunts that took place right after the Civil War were not always well organized. Sometimes the men would run short of food—and when that happened, they relied on the kindness of the women of nearby homes, as cowboy Luther Lawhon recalls in David Dary's book Cowboy Culture: A Saga of Five Centuries.

"[There was an] unwritten law, recognized by the good women of the towns as well as of the country, that whenever a party of cowhunters rode up and asked to have bread baked, it mattered not the time of day, the request was to be cheerfully complied with. . . . I remember the many times that cowhunters rode up to my father's house, and telling my mother they were out of bread, asked that she would kindly bake their flour for them. Everything was at once made ready. The sack was lifted from the pack horse and brought in, and in due time the bread wallets were once more filled with freshly cooked biscuits, and the cowboys rode away with grateful appreciation. These acts of consideration on the part of my mother were entirely gratuitous, but the generous-hearted cowboys would always leave either a half sack of flour or a money donation as a freewill offering."

cowpunchers he had known on many a drive and roundup past. The air echoed with greetings: "If it ain't . . . !" and "Well, I'll be!" Men with names like One-Eye Davis or Original John shouted friendly insults at friends named Curly Kid or Bean Belly.[80]

There would be no time for long conversations once the roundup started, for the men worked constantly, and any spare hours were used for sleeping.

The first day began early. At 3:30 A.M. the cook would ring a bell or loudly yell "Come and get it, boys!" At that hour, the air was still chilly, and the sky a grayish black. Even so, the men got up quickly, and stumbled over to the chuckwagon for a breakfast of strong coffee, biscuits, and gravy. After the meal, which usually the men were too tired to eat, the roundup began.

Sweeping the Range

The idea of the roundup seemed simple enough: each cowboy rode out from the center of camp (the center being where the chuck wagon was parked); when he had ridden seven miles, or ten, or whatever distance had been agreed upon, he turned around and headed back toward the center of camp.

As the cowboys rode, they herded all the cattle they could find toward the center. In fact, men left in camp could tell by the puffs of dust out on the prairie at just what moment the riders were beginning to find (and chase) the cattle.

The men wove back and forth, making a kind of "cowproof net" from which the cattle could not escape. A great deal of ground was covered—cowboys say that often they rode as much as seventy miles a day. Much of the

Cowboys ride back and forth to herd cattle. Roundups were hard on horses, who frequently broke their legs and had to be shot.

time the terrain was rocky and very rough. Cowboys rode through creek beds, down steep embankments searching for cattle that may have been hiding.

Such hard riding was tough on horses. It was not unusual for a horse to break a leg skidding down a hill on its haunches and, as a result, be shot by its rider. One visitor at a roundup witnessed such an incident, much to his horror.

An Easterner with a lively curiosity saw a spill down a steep hillside, when a horse thrust his foreleg down a gopher hole and threw his rider a distance the Easterner measured as "Thirty-seven feet less three inches." The cowboy was only slightly injured. He picked himself up, "and pulling his six-shooter forthwith, shot the disabled bronco."[81]

As the cowboys rode back and forth, tightening the invisible "net" around the cattle, the animals were driven in toward the center of camp. By the end of their riding, the cowboys had collected a herd of hundreds, sometimes thousands, of cattle. It was, as one cowboy recollects, "a dusty, milling, bawling herd of golden duns, murky yellows, reds, and piebalds."[82] The cows were a jumble of different brands, and of young calves born since the last roundup, who were not branded at all. The calves, of course, were the focus of the entire event.

A successful roundup was based on the assumption that calves follow their mothers. It was important, then, to separate the mothers from the herd so that their calves would come, too. After cowboys had identified the brands of the mothers, the calves could be marked with the correct brand. Separating cows from the safety of the herd was a tricky process called "cutting," which depended more on the skill of the horses than the riders.

A Horse Worth His Weight in Gold

Included in each cowboy's string of ponies provided by the rancher was one extraordinarily talented animal whose specialty was cutting. Of all the mounts a cowboy used, the cutting horse was the most valuable. A horse cannot be taught to cut cattle from a herd; those skills are somehow instinctive.

In any event, there is no time for a cowboy to give instructions during the cutting process, for the cow moves too fast. As one expert writes, a cowboy with a good cutting horse

could hold the reins at the end of his little finger, or perhaps let them lie over the saddlehorn. Once that cow pony knew, by some invisible twitch of the reins or by the pressure of a knee, what cow was wanted,

he would urge that animal with deceptive listlessness toward the rim of the herd, when with one sudden spring he could send the cow out at breakneck gait.[83]

The cowboy was an observer once he showed the horse with that "invisible twitch of the reins" which cow he wanted cut from the herd. After that signal, he watched as his horse made eye contact with the cow, using its body to scoot the cow away from the herd. Dodging and weaving, sometimes spreading its forelegs far apart to get down low, the little horse wheeled back and forth to prevent the cow from moving back to the herd. The cowboy's biggest challenge during this part of the roundup was simply not to fall out of the saddle.

A cutting horse is used to cut a steer from the herd for branding.

Eventually, the cow gave up, and most of the time her calf trotted along behind her. Of course, in all the yelling and confusion, it sometimes happened that a calf followed the wrong mother. As one cowboy writes, "In such cases, the cow herself adjusted the question of title by tossing the 'orphan' on her horns and returning to the [herd] to search for her rightful child."[84]

The Key to Ownership on the Range

Once the calf and its mother had been cut from the herd, the next step was to brand the young animal. Branding, says one historian, was "the key to ownership in a business where ownership was everything."[85] Branding was not invented by the cowboys—or even the *vaqueros*. Thousands of years ago, Egyptian breeders branded their herds to make identification easy.

There were hundreds of different brands, and each one was supposed to be registered with the county clerk. Some of the first ranchers started with an insignia bearing their initials, but as more and more people got into the ranching business, it was inevitable that duplicates would arise.

The need to create distinctive brands from a limited supply of markings forced cattle owners to be creative. A letter might be slanted and known as the "Lazy T," or given little feet and called the "Running W." Some ranchers used symbols such as a rocking chair or a frying pan. One man who had made a lot of money in a poker game used four 6's as the brand for his cattle. Another man with a devilish sense of humor used the symbol 2-ฺ-P, which was funny only when read out loud.

Many cowboys prided themselves on their ability to recognize the brands of various ranchers. And because there were hundreds of different brands in a given part of the state, such an accomplishment was pretty impressive. Even more impressive, say historians, was the ability to decipher old brands that had become hard to read on the hides of some cattle. Scarring and tufts of hair, as well as age, could make brands almost illegible to most people. But as one cowboy bragged, "A good cowboy could understand the Constitution of the United States were it written with a branding iron on the side of a cow."[86]

No Gentle Treatment

Having a distinctive brand registered at the county seat and actually searing into the flesh of a living calf were two different matters. Calves did not come willingly to the fire in the center of camp where the long irons were heating against the glowing coals. There were a number of ways by which they had to be "persuaded."

A newly branded calf is held down by the cowboy. Brands were unique and often creative.

A calf is roped from the hind feet while being branded. Branding was no gentle process, but necessary to claim ownership of the calf.

One way was by using a rope. Cowboys preferred to throw a "forefoot loop"—catching the calf's front feet. A calf roped this way could fall in a belly flop in the dirt but would rarely be hurt. A rope thrown over an animal's head, on the other hand, might yank the neck back, causing the calf to snap its neck and die as it fell.

Some cowboys liked to "bulldog" calves, a process that has been likened to "cow judo." In bulldogging, a cowboy would run or ride alongside a running calf, jump off his horse, and throw an arm over the calf's head. By giving the calf's head a quick turn, an experienced cowboy could use the animal's own momentum to drop it to the ground, as one observer wrote, "like a surprised wrestler."[87]

"Tailing" was another way of forcing a stubborn calf to the ground for branding. "Some of the tougher breed of cowboys thought nothing of grabbing a full-grown longhorn by the tail, twisting the appendage around a saddle horn, and dumping the luckless animal to the ground."[88] If tailing could work on a full-grown cow, it certainly worked on calves. There were many ranchers who disapproved of tailing, however, because they felt it was cruel and could possibly kill an animal.

The cowboys' treatment of the calves was no gentler once an animal had been captured and dragged to the branding fire, where one strong man flipped the calf on its side and held its head—or used a boot to hold its nose to the ground—while another applied the red-hot brand to the calf's side. The animal bawled in pain as its mother watched from a distance. Occasionally a protective mother would try to charge at the men, but other cowboys used ropes and horses to keep her back.

Not Painless

The process of branding was not a pleasant one, and most cowboys realized how painful it was. "I told one fellow if he would sit in his bare skin on a red hot stove for a minute," said cowboy D.J.O'Malley, "he could form a pretty good idea as to how a calf felt when a hot iron was putting a brand into his side."[89]

Other experts agree. "If there was one moment," wrote one Old West historian, "that stood out in the mind of the early Texas cowboy, it may have been the memory of putting the first hot iron to the flank of a calf."[90]

But the branding was not the only "surgery" done at the branding fire. Most ranchers also demanded that earmarks be cut on their cattle, as an extra means of identification. After all, brands could be doctored by cattle rustlers simply by inserting a bar above the registered symbol, or adding an initial. A notch on the side or the end of a cow's ear was one more way to prove ownership. There were more than two hundred different variations on the notches and cuts a rancher could use for his livestock. (Although horses were usually branded, they were not earmarked, for it was considered a disfigurement, and people were reluctant to "ruin" a good horse.)

The final bit of business was castration of male calves. Steers—that is, males whose testicles had been removed—were more likely to gain weight—a plus in the cattle business. Also, they were less likely to be aggressive with other males. One in ten male calves was left intact, however, for breeding purposes. After cutting off the testicles and throwing them in a bucket (there was a separate one for the ear clips), the cowboys let the calf loose, to run back to his mother.

This work was without glamor. One cowboy remembers the branding part of the roundup as a combination of "the bawling and the squirming of the calves and the bellowing of the watching cows . . . matched by the raucous shouts of men running about stripped to the waist and smeared with blood and dust, branding iron and knife in hand." He goes on to admit that the constant noise of the cattle and the shouting of men could be stressful, too, and a stressed cowboy could be cruel, especially when the frightened calf tried to fight back. "In an excess of temper not a part of his regular character, a cowboy hit by a flying hoof might retaliate with a vicious stab from his knife, or sink his spurred heel against the stomach of the offending calf."[91]

On Their Honor

Once an area had been swept of cattle, the camp was moved to a new area and the process was repeated until all the cattle in a district were accounted for. A tally man was appointed by the ranchers to keep an accurate count of the calves and full-grown cattle. The tally man was chosen because of his reputation as an honest man—and because he could read and write.

Disputes arose, nevertheless. Two ranchers might claim the same cow, each thinking the brand looked like his own. In these cases the argument was handled by the tally man, or by other ranchers participating in the roundup. As David Dary explains:

> [They] would find out what brand each one of the disputing parties were claiming the animal under, and if they could come to no agreement, the animal was roped, the brand moistened with water to make it plainer, or [they] would shear the hair off where the brand was located. . . . All this was done immediately, and then the work would proceed.[92]

Considering the numbers of men and animals involved in a roundup, however, it is amazing that there were not more arguments than there were. Most ranchers knew that they had to depend on one another. If a cow strayed too far from home, it was almost sure that another rancher would return the animal

Cowboys argue over the identification of a brand. Cattle rustlers often placed a similar brand on top of an existing brand, changing it slightly.

to its right place—even if it meant a journey of twenty miles. "Each cattleman and each cowboy under him was a man of honor," claimed another cowboy historian, "obligated to a course of equity in range business and fairness in human relations."[93]

There were plenty of opportunities to cheat during the course of a roundup. Calves could be quickly branded and set in the wrong herd, or cows could be "rebranded"

and taken over by another rancher. But most people were honest. In many cases, a man who couldn't attend the roundup would hand his brand over to his neighbors, certain that his calves would be properly branded and counted. Writes one cowboy proudly, "There are few businesses in which men have been more ready to assist one another than in the old cattle business of the range."[94]

Starting Up the Trail

Once all the cattle had been accounted for, a rancher could begin making plans for a trail drive north, for that was where the money could be made. A rancher could get about $4 per cow selling it for tallow and hide in Texas, but buyers in Kansas would pay ten times that amount.

A Long Journey

The trail drive was not a journey to be taken lightly. Depending on weather and the pace of the herd, a drive could last between three and four months. It was an event filled with every discomfort, hardship, and danger imaginable:

> There were swollen streams to swim, wild runs of cattle that had to be checked by a few men on tired mounts galloping over unknown land, perhaps bandits or Indians to face . . . and hardships that lacked even the virtue of the spectacular—drives all day in rain or mud, snatches of sleep on wet ground, sore and useless horses, bad cooking or none at all if brush and chips [fuel for cooking fires] were wet.[95]

But even with the discomforts and dangers, cowboys considered the trail drive the high point of each year. No self-respecting hand could call himself a cowboy until he had participated in one. "A cowboy is not a graduate in his art," one expert humorously remarks, "until he has been up the trail. His education has been sadly neglected if he has never taken a course in this, the highest, branch of bovine curriculum."[96]

Lots of Preparation

Preparing for a trail drive was a big job—one that has been compared to planning a military campaign. A rancher might decide to do the drive himself, although this was rare. Most ranchers could not afford to be away for months at a time, for there was too much to be done on the ranch. More often, a professional trail drive organizer, called a drover, was paid to supervise the journey. Usually the drover visited several neighboring ranchers and offered to buy cattle ready for market. If all went as planned, when the cattle were sold the drover would make a nice profit for himself.

Drovers almost never paid for the cattle until after the trail drive, but that presented no problem to the ranchers. According to historian Douglas Branch, "The stockowners knew that the [drover] needed all the money at his disposal to meet the expenses of the drive; they would not take a note for the purchase price, for honest men dealing with each other needed no notes."[97]

The size of the herd varied, but usually averaged about twenty-five hundred head. It might seem that smaller herds would be

Tricks on the Roundup

At the beginning of a trail drive, a second branding was often necessary, for there were almost always cattle from different ranches being taken to market. As one cowboy writes in The Cowboy Reader, *edited by Lon Tinkle and Allen Maxwell, the job of branding could be dangerous.*

"When everything came off right, a flanker could get hold of a calf, reach across his back, grab a handhold in his flank, give a yank as the calf jumped, roll him in the air, and bust him against the ground hard enough that the calf would lie there till the flanker could get on him, using his weight to hold the calf down.

But when something slipped, and it quite often did, then it was sometimes a hard matter to figure out which one was throwing which. Calf and man would get locked up, leg in arm, and around and around they'd go, with the calf bawling and the man swearing, and the iron man trying to fight them away from his branding fire.

Every cowhand knows that a calf is born with only four feet. But there are flankers who'll take a solemn cowhand oath that the minute you start to throw some calves, the animals sprout eight or ten extras. They claim that nothing with only four feet could kick so hard and so fast and from so many different directions all at once.

So many flankers have lost front teeth before this whirlwind of flailing hoofs that a gapped mouth has become a sort of trademark of the cowhand profession. In fact, some riders claim that a full set of front teeth is a distinct handicap in getting work at a new place. The wagon boss figures that a cowhand who's never had a tooth kicked out of his head is either short of experience or is a deadhead who won't step in and really take hold of the job."

Cowboys round up and brand calves on the range.

more manageable, but some cowboys felt that a few hundred cattle acted nervous and restless on a long journey. A larger herd usually meant safety. The largest trail drive in history, which took place in 1869, involved more than fifteen thousand cattle. That, say cowboys, was far too big an undertaking.

The Outfit

One of the expenses the drover assumed was hiring the trail boss, the man who would lead the trail drive. At about $150 per month, he was the highest paid member of the outfit. The trail boss was also the most experienced man, having participated in other drives. He would decide what trail to take, when to stop for the night, and what the pace would be. Not least of his responsibilities was to hire the cowboys needed to move the herds.

Cowboys received between $25 and $40 per month on a trail drive. For a drive involving 2,500 cattle, there would be about ten cowboys. The rule seemed to have been one man for every 250 or 300 cows.

The youngest man on the drive was undoubtedly the wrangler, the one in charge of the horses. Each cowboy had between five and nine extra horses for the journey—always a fresh horse when one became tired or sore. The group of horses was called the *remuda*, from the Spanish word meaning "remount." A good wrangler knew the name of every horse in the *remuda*, and the personality of each. He dreamed of being a cowboy himself, and watched every move the others made, so that he could learn enough to "move up" to cowboying. The wrangler was always the lowest paid member of the drive, getting about half of what cowboys made. For this small amount of money, he was expected to clean up after meals and run errands for the cook or the trail boss in addition to his duties with the horses.

A Man Called "Coosie"

Even though the trail boss's word was law on the drive, the cowboys felt that another member of the outfit was the most important. This was the cook, known by some as the Old Lady, Cookie, or, most affectionately, Coosie. A good cook was the key to a happy trail drive. Pleasures were so rare that food became all-important to the men. A grouchy cook, or one whose meals were boring or tasteless, had a tremendously negative effect on an outfit.

The cook was paid about $75 per month, and he earned every penny. No one worked longer or harder. He was always the first

A trail boss in the 1880s. Bosses were the most experienced men on the trail. They chose the trail and supervised the other cowboys.

A cowboy wrangler watches the horses that compose the remuda, *the spare horses. A wrangler was the lowest paid member of the team.*

man up in the morning—by 3:00 A.M. at the latest—and was often still working at midnight. He not only cooked, he packed and drove the chuckwagon, cut hair, doctored sick or injured cowboys, and sewed buttons. The cook was older than the others—usually a former cowboy himself who enjoyed life on the trail so much he couldn't give it up.

More Preparations

Once the outfit had been chosen and the financial deals agreed on by drover and ranchers, the cattle were checked to make certain they were all branded. If several ranchers' herds were being combined for a drive, the cattle were rebranded with a common brand to prevent confusion on the journey. Although the idea of branding so many cattle again must not have been a pleasant one, cowboys say that the "trail brand," as it was called, was a little easier to administer than the original. Because this mark did not have to be as deep and long lasting, it was not necessary to hold the branding iron against the cow's flank for as long.

The cowboys did very little in the way of preparation for a cattle drive. Space was at a minimum, so the men were allowed to bring only two blankets to make a bedroll, plus a little sack containing a change of pants and a shirt. Clean underwear and socks were not a priority.

The most preparation went into stocking the chuckwagon. Sometimes called "the trail drive's mother ship," or "a royal chamber on wheels," the chuckwagon was the backbone of the trail drive. Having a well-stocked chuckwagon was crucial in the success of the journey, and the drover and his assistants paid special attention to this area of preparation.

"The Trail Drive's Mother Ship"

The chuckwagon was the invention of Charles Goodnight, the first rancher in the Texas panhandle. In 1866 Goodnight wanted a mobile kitchen-pantry combination, one that could service his trail crews for up to four or five months at a time. He took a surplus army wagon—sturdy because of its durable iron axles—and customized it.

A cowboy cook works on the tailgate table of the chuckwagon. The hardest working member of the trail team, the cook was the first up in the morning and the last in bed at night.

The wagon had a canvas top for protection against wind and rain. There was plenty of room inside for the extra clothing and bedrolls the cowboys brought along. Goodnight also fastened a large water barrel on the side of the wagon. Water was a precious commodity on a trail drive, and the barrel had to be big enough for a two-day supply. A toolbox large enough to include shovel, ax, branding irons, extra pots and pans, and equipment for emergency horseshoeing was another necessity.

Under the wagon bed was a large piece of rawhide called the "possum belly," which was used to carry fuel for fires. To increase its size, the piece of rawhide was first stretched out with heavy rocks. Throughout the trail drive, it was the wrangler's job to keep the possum belly filled with pieces of kindling wood or cow chips. The latter were sometimes referred to as "prairie coal," for they burned with a hot, even flame. (Wranglers wore gloves when collecting the cow chips, for it was firmly believed that there was a scorpion living under each one.)

The most innovative aspect of Goodnight's design was the chuck box, a large chest of drawers built at the rear of the wagon. This big cabinet contained more than a dozen compartments, drawers, and cubbyholes. One was for flour and sugar, another for fruit and beans. One was for the cook's spices, another for coffee. A drawer held a needle, thread, razors, and other odds and ends. One cubbyhole was for medicines, which usually meant a stash of whiskey. Alcohol was strictly forbidden to the cowboys on trail drives, but a bottle was in the control of the cook, who helped himself to a sip or two frequently, according to historians.

Goodnight's chuck box had a hinged lid, which could be transformed into a worktable

Charles Goodnight, inventor of the chuckwagon, went from being a cowboy to owning his own herd.

cattle owners copied the idea, and soon the Studebaker Company produced and sold the chuckwagons for $75 apiece throughout the West.

Setting the Pace

The final decision of the route to be taken to Kansas was left to the trail boss. From 1868 on the choice was fairly easy—the Chisholm Trail was the most popular, although other routes were used as well. The Chisholm Trail was named after Jesse Chisholm, a Scottish-Cherokee scout who had laid out a supply route from Texas to Kansas during the Civil War. After the war, many cowboys used the same route.

The Chisholm Trail was between two hundred and four hundred yards wide, and after a few years—and a few million hooves—it had become so worn down that like a dusty river, it ran lower than the surrounding plains. Chisholm had chosen the path at first because it had good grazing land alongside it, and ample watering holes between Kansas and Texas.

There was no "official" beginning to a drive. No one cracked a whip or gave a signal to begin. The cattle were allowed to drift at first, grazing and drinking water. Soon, however, the more aggressive ones—usually steers—took their places at the front of the huge herd, and remained there for the entire trail drive.

The cattle moved in line in order of assertiveness. The aggressive cattle were followed by mothers and their calves, then older cattle. The last in line were the animals that were lame, lazy, or, as some cowboys described them, "just plain stupid."

Although every herd of cattle had at least one leader, some trail bosses preferred to

Cowboys make their meals at the chuckwagon's folding table. The wagon's various cubbyholes and compartments can be seen as well.

when the lid was fastened to a swinging leg. The worktable was a lifesaver for the cook, for space to mix and chop was at a premium on the trail. But, say cowboys, woe to the cowboy who was foolish enough to try to eat at the worktable. Writes one cowboy, "Any greenhorn who tried to use it for a dining table would be called names that would peel the hide off a Gila monster."[98]

Charles Goodnight's chuckwagon, according to one historian, was "unique at the time, and a useful prototype for all self-respecting wagons that followed."[99] Before long other bring in a veteran—one who had led a previous drive and done well. The most famous of the veterans was named Old Blue, owned by Texas rancher Charles Goodnight. Old Blue was a good leader, and a calming influence on the other cattle. He wore a brass bell around his neck, and the other cattle learned to follow him. Writes one historian, "He never shied at sudden disturbances and disdained to take part in stampedes."[100]

Goodnight relied on Old Blue for eight seasons. During that time he led an estimated ten thousand cattle north to Kansas—sometimes twice a year. When Old Blue died, at the age of twenty, his horns were given a place of honor in a Texas museum honoring cowboys.

A Pecking Order for Cowboys, Too

As the herd slowly lumbered into motion, the cowboys got into their own formation. The two most experienced cowboys were called "point men," and they rode at the front of the herd. Their job was to guide the progress of the cattle and set the pace. It was important that the cattle not walk so quickly that they lost weight, for they were sold by the pound.

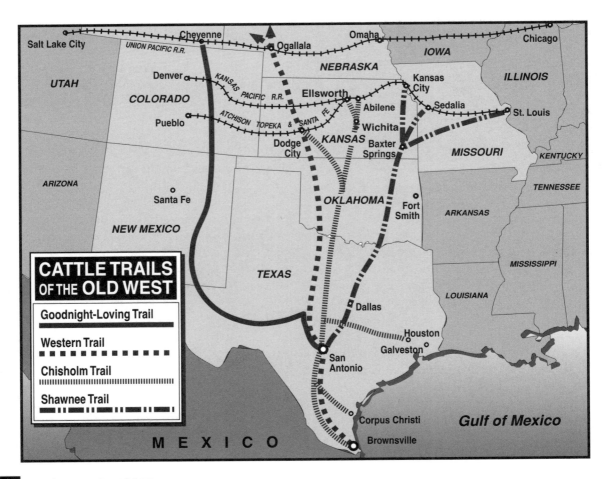

The formation of the cattle drive can be seen clearly here, as can the vast number of cattle stretching to the horizon.

At the sides of the herd were the "swing men," followed by "flank riders," who kept the cattle from straying off to one side or another, or from lagging behind and creating gaps in the herd. Another function of the swing men and flank riders was to keep out "extras." These were cattle grazing nearby, which might be tempted to join in as the large herd drifted past. While extras would increase the herd size, it would not do for their owner to discover his missing cattle on another rancher's trail drive.

The worst job among the cowboys was "drag riding." The drag riders followed the herd, shooing along cattle that refused to keep going. These were the men who literally choked on the dust kicked up by the thousands of hooves dragging across the trail. A drag rider's most important piece of equipment was his bandanna, for that lessened somewhat the effects of the blizzard of dust. "I've seen drag riders come off herd with the

dust half an inch deep on their hats and thick as fur in their eyebrows," writes cowboy Teddy Blue Abbott. "If they shook their head or you tapped their cheek, the dust would fall off them in showers." [101]

To keep the slow or lame cattle from stopping in their tracks, drag riders relied on their lariats, using them like whips. Writes one historian:

[The drag rider's] lariat thrusts were truly stablike inasmuch as, having spliced a long buckskin "popper" on the home end of his rope, he, by an underhanded throw with a snap of his wrist, could "shoot" that popper and the twenty feet of rope behind it, and this . . . either cut into the hide of a steer or else made a sound like a pistol.[102]

The trail boss did not stay with the herd, but instead rode ahead to scout out good grazing, watering, and bedding places. These locations were never directly alongside a trail; they could be a mile or more away. Because of the constant zigzagging necessary in finding good places for grass and water, the trail boss might ride forty miles each day, while the herd moved ten to fifteen.

Setting Off

But although a pace of ten to fifteen miles per day was standard, cowboys preferred to cover a lot more territory in the first few days. This was called "getting the herd trail-broke," and a "trail-broke" herd made cowboys' jobs much easier. The cowboys would herd the cattle along quickly at first, to move them out of familiar territory. Otherwise, they would wander off, not understanding that there was a journey to be made. Besides, traveling great distances in the first few days tired the cattle out, and this usually made them a bit more manageable.

By noon each day the herd had traveled about five miles. The trail boss and the cook had agreed earlier on a suitable place to camp

for lunch. It was not a long stop—never more than an hour—but the men had a chance to eat something (almost always potluck—odds and ends) and the cattle and horses could graze.

The drive continued all afternoon until about 5:00, when the men would eagerly watch for the trail boss to appear, waving his hat slowly. That was the signal for the cowboys to make camp for the night. The point men and swing men slowed the herd down, which the cattle understood was permission to graze. As the herd grazed, the flank riders and swing men forced the cattle into circles. The cattle bunched closer and closer together, and then began to lie down.

The wrangler quickly constructed a corral out of ropes, to confine the *remuda* for the night. Since the cowboys took turns watching the cattle during the night, however, each one would remove his "night horse," the one with the best vision, from the corral. Most cowboys used a technique called "hobbling" to make sure their horses didn't run away at night. Hobbling involved tying the horse's front legs together with a leather cuff. A hobbled horse

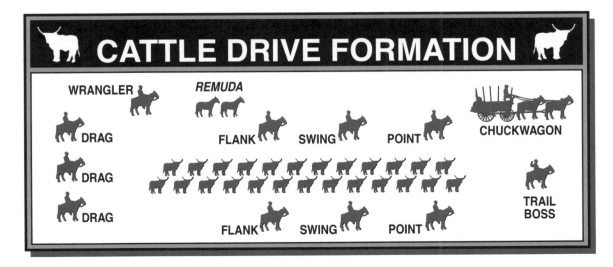

Horses in the remuda *are kept in a makeshift corral and guarded by the wranglers.*

moved around, but could not get very far from the camp while his rider slept.

Son-of-a-Bitch Stew and Other Entrées

The cowboys who did not have the first shift watching the cattle gathered at the camp. By this time, the cook had started his fire, and preparations for dinner were well under way. Trail driving was long, hard, dirty work. The only real pleasure the men had was eating, so food took on huge importance.

The cowboy's diet on the trail was pretty monotonous, however, for the cook was limited to items that could be stored for many weeks at a time—as well as to foods that could be cooked in the cramped quarters of his chuckwagon. There were plenty of beans, dried apples, and salt pork, called "sowbelly." Occasionally, the trail boss might strike a bargain with a nearby rancher for some eggs and fresh vegetables. For example, a farmer might request that the cattle be bedded in his fields so that he could

have the cow chips for fertilizer and fuel. In other cases a farmer supplied groceries in exchange for a calf born on the drive. The cowboys would have had to shoot the calf anyway, since a newborn couldn't keep up, so getting the fresh farm food was a real bonus.

One would think that because cows were what the trail drive was all about, there would be plenty of beef, but that was not always so. "Killing a beef [cow] on the trail was a great waste," commented one cowboy in his journal, "as only a small part of the meat could be eaten before it spoiled."[103] The trail boss would never approve of slaughtering one of the animals they were taking to market—it was depriving the crew of money when they reached Kansas. Instead, they might kill a cow that joined the herd along the way, one that was missed by the flankers, or one that the drag riders declared to be hopelessly lame.

The favorite use for beef on a trail drive was a true cowboy concoction known as son-of-a-bitch stew. Cooks claimed that it contained "everything but hair, horns, and holler," and judging by the parts of the cow used, they weren't exaggerating by much. Son-of-a-bitch stew contained the tongue, heart, brains, and kidneys of a young cow—not more than a year old. The ingredient that gave the stew its distinct flavor was marrow gut—not a gut at all, but rather a tube connecting the compartments of a cow's stomach.

One expert in Old West cooking states that marrow gut is good "only when the calf is young and living upon milk, as [the tube] is then filled with a substance resembling marrow through which the partially digested milk passes. . . . The marrow-like contents were left in, and they were what gave the stew such a delicious flavor."[104]

The strange stew became a rite of passage for true cowboys, separating them from the greenhorns or "tenderfeet." Sometimes, too, it was used by a veteran cowhand to amuse himself at a newcomer's expense. As one historian writes, "When [an old-timer] watched some greener picking around in a plate of this mysterious looking stew as if trying to discover its ingredients, he would remark that a stew was no good without plenty of *guts* in it. If the tenderfoot grew pale and pushed the dish aside, his reward was ample."[105]

Frying Up Some "Bear Sign"

One of the most welcome "treats" a camp cook could make for the crew was doughnuts. In his book Come an' Get It: The Story of the Old Cowboy Cook, *Ramon Adams describes the excitement on the trail drive among the cowboys when the cook began making them.*

"On rare occasions, if time hung heavily on his hands and he was filled with good cheer, the cook would 'fry up' some doughnuts—'bear sign,' he called them. This was indeed a treat for the boys, and an outfit which had a cook who could and would make an occasional batch of 'bear sign' was the envy of the entire range.

If any of the boys were [around] when this event was taking place, they crowded around to watch these tasty rings of dough browning in the bubbling grease until they became a tantalizing brown. Scarcely had the cook forked them from the grease and placed them in a waiting pan when eager hands reached out to empty it. The grunts of admiration, the smacking of lips, and the licking of grease from fingertips was music to the cook. He let the boys consume the first three or four fryings without comment, but when he thought they had had enough, he moved the pan where he would be between it and the boys.

'That's 'nough, boys,' he'd say. 'Don't make a damned hawg of yo'self. Save some for the other boys.'

As he shooed them away from the kitchen, there would be some mild grumbling, but beneath it all was a deep satisfaction, for a 'bear sign' was indeed an occasion which made the boys love old coosie with a fierce loyalty."

"Who Wants the Candy Tonight?"

Most cowboys loved coffee, and the trail cook made sure there was a good supply at all times. The brand used on trail drives was Arbuckle's, and it had to be ground by hand before it could be brewed. However, as Ramon Adams explains in his book, Come an' Get It: The Story of the Old Cowboy Cook, *the cook seldom had to do the grinding himself.*

"This coffee was shipped in cases of one-pound bags. The ranch owner kept a supply on hand at all times. When the chuck wagon loaded out for the roundup, plenty of coffee was taken along. There was no stinting on this item if the men were to do good work and be contented.

Its gaily colored manila bag was a familiar sight at the chuck wagon. . . . At the bottom of the package was a coupon which helped this brand of coffee to become so well known. This was the facsimile of the signature 'Arbuckle Brothers,' printed in red on a white-splotched background and bordered in black. At one time a stick of striped peppermint candy was packed in every sack. If the wrangler happened to be busy and the cook was out of ground coffee, he would merely ask, 'Who wants the candy tonight?' and there would be a rush for the coffee grinder fastened to the side of the wagon. Perhaps while two or three men were scuffling to keep each other away from the grinder handle, another would slip past them and grind the coffee."

Vinegar Pie and Six-Shooter Coffee

Dessert on the trail was usually canned fruit—raisins, apples, or prunes. If the cook was in a good mood, the crew might be treated to pie. Writes one expert, "A cowboy would go to hell for a piece of pie."[106] The cook who occasionally treated his boys to pie was a treasure, every trail boss knew.

The pies were simple: fruit surrounded by thick crust on top and bottom. Although many cowboys liked fancy toppings such as meringue (which they called "calf slobber"), the scarcity of eggs made them impossible. One of the most common pies made on the drive was called vinegar pie. The cook used a quarter of a pint of vinegar, water, and enough sugar to sweeten the taste. He added this to a lump of fat frying in a skillet, then put the whole mixture between strips of rolled dough. Many cowboys thought vinegar pie was the best dessert imaginable.

Meals ended with coffee—a staple on a trail drive. Cowboys consumed quarts of coffee each day. They relied on it as more than a beverage, as one historian writes. "Men going out on guard needed a cup of coffee to keep them awake; those being relieved needed a cup when they rode in to warm them up before resuming their interrupted sleep. And no matter how short his sleep, the cowboy wanted another cup immediately upon arising."[107]

Like good meals, coffee was a rare pleasure on a bleak job, and the cook who made sure there was always enough earned the men's respect:

> It was said that if there was anything that a cowpuncher liked better than a fiddler in camp, it was drinking coffee between meals. The cook who kept the coffeepot over a bed of hot coals during the day and night would find that the boys were "for him."[108]

Cowboys liked their coffee strong—nothing like the stuff they called "brown

Cowboys sing on the trail when the day's work is done. Singing was important not only for entertainment, but also because it calmed the cattle.

gargle" served in town at restaurants. They called their coffee "six-shooter coffee," because it was said to be strong and thick enough to float a six-shooter. There was a well-known recipe cooks jokingly credited with turning out the best coffee on earth: "Take one pound of coffee, wet it good with water, boil it over a fire for 30 minutes, pitch in a horseshoe, and if it sinks, put in some more coffee."[109]

Putting milk in coffee was a sign of weakness on a trail drive. To the cowboy, having breath that smelled like a calf's was unthinkable. Sugar was not used in coffee, either, but for different reasons. It was impossible to keep in restaurant-type dispensers, for moisture hardened it into unusable lumps, and ants got the rest. Thus, the first cowboys in the Old West never saw sugar, and those who followed didn't see it often.

If a cowboy wanted his coffee a little sweeter, he used molasses. One cowboy had a friend who went to a fancy roundup camp at dinnertime. The sugar was passed, but never having seen it before, the friend said, "No thanks, I don't take salt in my coffee."[110]

Night on the Trail

After dinner the men not on guard duty relaxed around the campfire. They told jokes, engaged in conversations about people they had met, or discussed experiences on other drives. Often, the idea was not so much to relate true accounts as to "outdo" other men's stories. If someone had stored a fiddle in the chuckwagon, or had brought a little harmonica, there was singing. Some of the men rolled cigarettes; others began setting out their bedrolls on the ground. They would sleep until they were wakened for their shift of guard duty.

Out a little way from camp, the two men on guard rode in a large circle, one going counterclockwise, the other clockwise. Their job was to make sure the cattle were calm and had no reason to move. The herd usually lay quietly at night, moving only around midnight, when they all got to their feet and lay down again in a new position.

The best way to keep the herd quiet and calm was to sing to them. Some men swore that certain herds responded best to hymns; others used love songs. For most cowboys, however, it didn't seem to matter what words or melody, as long as the cattle could hear the calming sound of a man's singing voice.

So important was singing to a cowboy on the trail drive, in fact, that many trail bosses wouldn't hire a man who couldn't sing. For the better part of a two-hour shift, each man sang every song he knew—and faked it through several he did not. Some popular tunes were "Dinah Had a Wooden Leg," "The Unfortunate Pup," "The Old-Time Cowboy," and "The Old Chisholm Trail." When these were used up, say cowboys, anything sung softly and soothingly would usually work. Writes one historian:

When weary of singing the same old songs, the night herders invented new verses, sometimes chanting with deep religious fervor a string of disconnected profanity, or the text from a label of Arbuckle's coffee, or perhaps an unflattering discourse on the habits of Longhorns.[111]

The cook would be busy for another few hours after the men went to sleep, rolling out new batches of dough for the next day's sourdough biscuits. After midnight—sometimes as late as 2:00 A.M.—the cook finished his work. After the first day's very early start, he had to be awake by 4:00 the same morning, although he could climb in his chuckwagon during the day to nap while the other men were working.

The cook's last task each night was to turn the wagon tongue toward the North Star. Compasses were not used by cowboys; instead, they told directions solely by the stars. The cook would put a lighted lantern on the wagon tongue so that in the dark hours of early morning, the guard shift could find its way safely back to camp.

A number of problems prevented the cowboys on a trail drive from slipping into a routine. Even though many days on the trail were uneventful, trouble and danger were constant threats—to cowboys and cattle alike.

Rustlers and Other Dangers

Some of the most dangerous hazards faced by Texas trail drivers were human. Cattle rustlers would stampede a herd on purpose, and afterward collect the strays and claim them. In the Indian Territory, an area that is now Oklahoma, Native American nations such as the Cherokee were angry about cattle drives across their land. They had their own cattle and did not want thousands of strange animals passing through, depleting the grazing land.

To even the score, Cherokees along one well-used trail charged trail drivers a toll of 10 cents a head for crossing through their land. They enforced the toll by means of a highly organized police patrol called the Cherokee Light Horse. Most of the time trail drivers found it easier to pay the toll, for they were ill prepared for a fight.

The most violent encounters faced by cowboys in the early years of the trail drive were with farmers in Missouri and Kansas who knew the Texas cattle carried ticks that caused "Texas fever." Although the long-

Cattle rustlers fight off a posse. Rustlers were one of the main dangers on the trail.

Locoweed on the Prairie

Cowboys had to keep an eye on the kind of grass their stock was grazing on, for sometimes it could be poisonous. As one man from England who came to Texas to become a cowboy found out, a horse eating locoweed dies an agonizing death—as related in William H. Forbis's book The Cowboys. *The herd of horses entrusted to his care had eaten the weed, and were lying on the ground, groaning and foaming at the mouth.*

"Having shot two horses which were unable to stand up, we rounded up our cripples and made a start for the headquarters ranch 180 miles due south. In addition to being badly locoed and half-starved, the majority suffered a skin disease which eats the hair off and leaves the shivering creature exposed. Many of them had open kidney sores and wither-galls, swollen running nostrils, watering eyes, and wheezy breathing. Three long weeks did this melancholy procession trail across the prairie.

Every now and then a horse stumbled and fell; generally he was too weak to rise, when a couple of boys dismounted, and, passing a rope under his body and round his shoulders, hoisted the poor beast on his legs again. As a rule this was the beginning of the end, if he managed to hold up until the end of the day's march, the frosty night settled him. Every morning in the chill half-light of early dawn, it was our sad duty to lift those who had lain down to rest, and, by rubbing their stiffened trembling limbs, to restore circulation sufficiently to enable them to stand. Others were beyond help, and several times I have given such their quietus with a six-shooter bullet without drawing more than faint trickle of blood, so poor were they."

---

horns themselves were immune to the disease, the range cattle of Kansas and Missouri that came into contact with the longhorns sickened and died. Some of the farmers allowed the trail drivers to cross their land only if they paid exorbitant fees. However, most farmers armed themselves with shotguns and fired on Texas herds trying to cross their land; many cowboys and cattle were killed.

The state legislatures of Kansas and Missouri hurriedly passed laws in 1866 to establish quarantines in certain sections of their states, and to prohibit the herds from Texas from entering their borders until after the summer, when the fever was not a problem because the ticks were dormant. Tens of thousands of cattle were backed up in Baxter Springs, Kansas, that summer waiting to complete their drive. The grass grew thin, then nonexistent, as the hungry cattle looked frantically for something to eat.

Meanwhile, the Texas trail drivers grew more and more anxious, as they watched their cattle starve. The animals that survived looked more like skeletons than cattle. The trail bosses, desperate to unload their herds, accepted any offer for the cattle—including some written as bad checks.

Although Texas fever continued to plague range cattle north of Texas, the problems between cattlemen and farmers diminished after that. As the railroad inched its way west and south, it was no longer necessary to go through the parts of Kansas and Missouri that were quarantined. But, say historians, it is amazing that the next year there were trail drives at all, for most ranchers in 1866 lost money on the venture. Cowboys in later years sarcastically advised one another to stay out of Kansas altogether, since there was so much hostility directed at trail herders passing through. "Nothing in Kansas anyhow," they joked, "except the three suns—sunflowers, sunshine, and those sons-of-bitches." [112]

Watering the Herd

In the years after the disastrous year of 1866, as dangers from humans lessened somewhat, nature continued to provide obstacles to the trail drivers. One of the biggest problems on a drive was keeping the herds watered. In fact, one of the chief responsibilities of the trail boss was to locate watering sites along the way. This often kept him away from camp for an extra thirty or forty hours at a time, sometimes riding more than a day ahead of the herd.

It was not always enough that the trail boss had ridden the trail before. What had been excellent watering holes last trip might be muddy ditches during times of drought. In scouting for water, a trail boss often relied on the behavior of swallows—if the birds were swooping around carrying mud in their beaks for nests, chances were that a watering hole was nearby.

Cattle traveling in herds needed more water than the wild longhorns. Perhaps it was the rigorous pace of their forced march, or the tons of dust that choked them as they moved. Whatever the reason, cowboys knew that their herds needed to be watered once

every day or two. A longer time without water meant trouble.

Cattle can smell water—from as far away as ten or fifteen miles. Once they catch the scent, hot, thirsty cattle that had been moving listlessly could move very quickly. As one historian writes, if "there was no sign of water, cattle would become restless and ill-tempered; but with the first smell of water the lead cattle, always the most acute, began to bellow, and quickened their pace." [113]

An old cowboy describes the strange movement of thirsty cattle. "Their necks were stretched and mouths open with continued bawling. It looks like a walking race; they shuffle along with the most busy determination, careless of [everything] but the getting over the ground." [114]

But sometimes the cattle headed for a river or creek with dangerous speed. As their trotting became galloping, and then stampeding, a herd running for water became an

A longhorn cattle drive from Texas. To reach Kansas such drives had to cross farmland. Farmers were wary of the wild cattle, which often gave their own cattle diseases.

unstoppable force. There are many stories of cattle trampling one another, or goring one another with their sharp horns, as they ran. In such circumstances, when water was finally reached, the lead cattle that stopped to drink were trampled by those behind. In 1871 a rancher lost three hundred head of cattle in a river, crushed by those that followed them.

"They Became Feverish and Ungovernable"

At times when the heat sizzled the trail and the sun beat down relentlessly, thirsty cattle simply refused to go on. Instead of continuing northward, they turned, trying to head back to the last watering hole they'd used—perhaps days before. Old-time cowboy Andy Adams writes of the cowboys' frustration in trying to keep cattle from turning back:

> Over three days had now elapsed without water for the cattle, and they became feverish and ungovernable. The lead cattle turned back several times, wandering aimlessly in any direction, and it was with considerable difficulty that the herd could be held on the trail. The rear overtook the lead, and the cattle gradually lost all semblance of a trail herd . . . milling and lowing in their fever and thirst . . . ungovernable as the waves of an ocean.[115]

Finally, Adams writes, the cattle were simply too powerful to be contained. The cowboys panicked, refusing to let them lose several days' ground by returning to a previous watering hole. They threw ropes in the cattle's faces, and even fired their six-shooters "so close to the leaders' faces as to singe their hair, yet, under a noonday sun, they disre-garded this and every other device to turn them, and passed wholly out of control." Adams remembers that some of the steers deliberately walked into the cowboys' horses—something they normally never did—and "a fact dawned on us that chilled the marrow in our bones—*the herd was going blind*."[116]

Swelling and blackening of the tongue, temporary blindness—these are signs of cattle dangerously close to death from dehydration. In Adams's case, the herd was finally allowed to turn back the way it wanted to go, and luckily all cattle survived. Other cowboys, far less fortunate, watched helplessly as blind cattle stumbled and died, victims of the uncertainty of the trail.

The Science of Watering Cattle

"I have met but few men," writes one old-time rancher, "who knew how to water cattle properly."[117] It was not enough to locate water and lead the cattle to it. Besides making sure the animals didn't trample one another, it was important to keep the first ones to drink at a stream or creek from turning it into a muddy hole for those who followed.

After all, not only cattle used the water. There was an established order to the use of water, starting with the cook, who watered his team of horses and then filled the barrel on the chuckwagon. After that, the *remuda* was watered, followed by the cattle. Finally, when they had finished drinking, the cowboys were allowed their turn.

If the cowboys and trail boss did a poor job of keeping the cattle out of the water, they would all suffer. "I ain't kickin'" one cowboy recalled, "but I had to chew that water before I could swaller it."[118] Historians of the Old West maintain that praise for their

Cowboys bathe in a watering hole. Cowboys were allowed into the watering hole only after the cook, the remuda, *and the cattle had taken their share.*

skill at watering herds was one of the highest compliments a trail crew could receive.

In *We Pointed Them North*, cowboy Teddy Blue Abbott recalled two veteran trail hands he knew who were experts at watering. They could, says Abbott, water two thousand cattle at a spring that was "about as big as a wagon box." By keeping the cattle back, and bringing up a few at a time to drink, he says, they kept the watering hole clean and clear for everyone. Writes Abbott, "It was the slickest piece of cow work I ever saw in my life."[119]

"One Jump to Their Feet, the Second to Hell"

The cowboy's worst nightmare on a trail drive was a stampede: "spooked" cattle running mindlessly, trampling everything in their path. The most deadly stampede in history happened in 1876 when a big herd thundered into a gully near the Brazos River in Texas. The cattle in front were crushed by those following; more than two thousand head were killed or missing when the stampede was over. Stampedes were a frightening fact of life on drives in the Old West, but they were especially common in the early days after the Civil War, when longhorns—known to be restless and nervous—made up the majority of herds.

The stampedes were not only dangerous to the men and the cattle, they could be financially disastrous. As cattle ran, they lost weight at an incredible rate—sometimes fifty pounds in one run of several miles. Often, too, cattle ran so far that they became lost. When there were missing cattle, cowboys had to go looking for them, which took up valuable time. Cowboys and ranchers made their money by delivering every cow in the herd, at top weight. Thus a stampede or two along the way meant money lost.

One old-time trail boss named George Duffield led a drive from Texas in 1866. In brief, frustrated little journal entries, he indicates that the aftermath of a stampede was very discouraging. On May 1, he wrote, "Big stampede. Lost 200 head of cattle." On May 2: "Spent the day hunting and found but 25 head. It has been raining for three days. These are dark days for me . . . hunted all day and the rain pouring down with but poor success. . . . Nothing but bread and coffee, hands all growling and swearing—everything wet and cold." And a full two weeks later, on May 16, he wrote, "Hunt Beeves [plural of beef, a cowboy word for "cow"] is the word—all hands discouraged and are determined to go. 200 Beeves out and nothing to eat." [120]

Cowboys were never sure why herds stampeded. The causes varied from the understandable to the absurd. According to one expert, a herd could start running because

sheep had suddenly been seen or scented, or blood had been smelled, or a man's hat had blown off, or a pack of cards had been tossed by the wind, or a horse or rider had loudly sneezed, or a night horse had shaken its saddle, or a tin can had been dropped . . . or rain or hail

The Treachery of Quicksand

One of the most dangerous of all natural hazards encountered on a trail drive was quicksand. In his book Some of the Old-Time Cowmen of the Great West, *author Usher L. Burdick explains some of the fine points of crossing an area of quicksand, as told by cowboys themselves.*

"It was necessary to ford many streams with cattle and wagons during the early Western days. At first the cowboy's inclination was to rush through quicksand with both the cattle and rolling stock, and a great number of them never learned that there should be different methods employed. Ed Lemmon agrees that the crossing of wagons must not lag, for if permitted to settle in the sand, all is lost. However, this is not true of livestock. Horses and cattle should be allowed to take the sand in a slow and easy manner, and if fatigued, can be rested without danger in most cases. The life motion of legs of animals will 'lob-lolley' the quicksand, preventing the potent suction force which operates on rolling stock.

Ed once crossed the Pine Creek with a round-up crew who forced their horses so hard that they finally bogged down. He suggested that they take it easy as he was doing, but his advice was not heeded for he was but a youngster to the others. Ed was the only one who did not bog down but his successful crossing was attributed to the ability of his horse to wriggle out. However, he was thereafter detailed to oversee crossings of both wagons and cattle. He frequently found it expedient to cross the cattle first, and then follow with the wagons over the relatively safe path through the quicksand which had thus been made."

had abruptly either begun or ceased, or the moon had suddenly appeared from behind a hill, or any one of a thousand and one things had occurred.[121]

One cowboy recalled a stampede that began when a speck of his chewing tobacco lodged in the eye of one of the lead steers. That set off a stampede that killed four hundred cows and two cowboys. Another stampede was caused by a steer that had one odd eye and crooked horns—characteristics that evidently frightened the other cattle. Many cowboys were convinced that certain herds just had a chemistry that made them want to stampede, and they would do it again and again. Said one cowboy of such herds, "They would rather run than eat, anytime."[122]

Whatever the reason, the cause of the stampede and its beginning happened almost simultaneously. Cowboys had a phrase, "One jump to their feet, the second to hell," to describe how quickly the cattle jumped up from a lying-down position and began galloping. A herd of more than a thousand rose as one animal and began to run at top speed immediately. They did not bellow or bawl—quite the contrary. The only noise in a stampede was the rumbling of the earth as they moved. "The longhorns, though angular and ungainly to look at," writes one historian, "ran with surprising speed, their hooves pounding and their horns clashing as they thundered along."[123]

"Beef Against Horseflesh"

Although stampedes could happen at any time, the most frightening were those that occurred at night. A cowboy might be awakened by a frantic yell from one of the men on guard duty: "Cattle are running—all hands!"

No one needed to be told twice. Every man on the drive, with the exception of the cook in the chuckwagon, grabbed his night horse. (Many cowboys hobbled their night horses next to them; a few even slept holding the reins loosely in one hand.) The cattle could not be allowed to run unchecked. For the next several hours, predicted experienced cowboys, it would be "beef against horseflesh, with the odds on the beef for the first hundred yards."

The object for cowboys was to outrun the herd. Once they had caught up with the leaders, the cowboys would try to swing them around—either by riding tight next to the lead steer, or by yelling or firing their pistols

A cowboy attempts to outrun a stampeding herd in order to swing it into a circle.

Stampede!

Stampedes were always frightening, dangerous occurrences on a trail drive. In his book Some of the Old-Time Cowmen of the Great West, *Usher Burdick recounts a stampede that cowboys feel caused more damage than any other.*

"The most destructive stampede [cowboy Ed] Lemmon ever witnessed was during the time seven herds of old Longhorn cattle were being held and peddled out. One night during a storm one of the herds stampeded and all of the others, including Ed's, followed suit. Ed and his Mexican crew jumped to their horses and were soon nearing the lead of the cattle, but it was impossible to stop them when the rumble of another stampeding herd across a gulch came to their hearing.

The rumble of two thousand head of stampeding cattle is similar to the rumble of a freight train, and the vibration frightens the cattle as much as the noise itself. It is natural for stampeding herds to draw together if one can scent the other. In this instance, unfortunately, there was a deep gulch between the two onrushing herds, as was soon discovered when the black mass in front of the men dropped from view. The men quickly spread out and let the cattle go by, just managing to prevent being swept on with the stampede.

As the cattle plunged headlong into the gorge the noise of pounding hoofs was terrific and the ground shook as during an earthquake. The night was oppressively dark, but the herd could be traced by the electric sparks which blazed from their horns. Suddenly there was a deafening roar and a severe quaking which threatened to upset the riders. The two herds of cattle had crashed headlong in the gorge.

Not until dawn were the men fully aware of the extent of this tragic occurrence. The dead and mangled stock formed an enormous bridge in the gorge; it was a horrible thing to behold. A great deal of time was spent skinning the carcasses which the health authorities required to be buried."

near the heads of the cattle. If they could get the herd to circle, or mill, the animals would eventually slow down.

However, the process of milling the herd was dangerous for the crew. As one expert writes, "The situation called for a dashing, swearing daredevil, with a horse unafraid to gallop in the dark over unknown country, as eager to end the stampede as his rider."[124] Riding alongside a stampeding herd was hot work, for the cattle's bodies generated blistering heat as they ran.

But the discomfort of breathing the hot, dusty air was small in comparison to the danger posed by the treacherous surface the cowboys had to ride over. Rocks, ravines, and especially prairie dog holes were wicked obstacles for a cowboy galloping full speed in total darkness. It is true that night horses were known for their keen eyesight, but there were limits to their abilities. The journals and diaries of cowboys and trail bosses in the Old West are filled with sad tales of friends and coworkers killed in stampedes.

One historian writes that the aftermath of a stampede was always a little scary, as cowboys took a quick roll call to see if anyone was missing:

> This was done with anxiety which always was as tender in spirit as it was flippant in form. The riders, returning one by one during the next day's morning hours, came into camp, and an atmosphere of banter—banter which, in joking phrases . . . ran on one occasion somewhat as follows: "Hulloa, Shorty, where'd you come from? Thought you was dead. . . . Where's Baldy? Guess he's gone off to git married. . . . No, he ain't. Here he comes."[125]

Sometimes, however, the banter stopped quickly when it was evident that one of the cowboys was indeed missing. Teddy Blue Abbott recalls a stampede in which a man died:

> We went back to look for him, and we found him among the prairie dog holes, beside his horse. The horse's ribs was scraped bare of hide, and all the rest of horse and man was mashed into the ground as flat as a pancake. The only thing you could recognize was the handle of his six-shooter. We tried to think the lightning hit him, and that was what we wrote his folks down in Henrietta, Texas. But we couldn't really believe it ourselves. I'm afraid it wasn't the lightning. I'm afraid his horse stepped into one of them holes and they both went down before the stampede. We got a shovel—I remember it had a broken handle—and we buried him nearby, on a hillside. . . . But the awful part of it was that we had milled them cattle over him all night, not knowing he was there. . . . And after that,

orders were given to sing when you was running with a stampede, so the others would know where you were.[126]

Taking Precautions

Regardless of whether cowboys had died in a stampede, the crew was angry afterward. A head count was taken of the herd, and all missing animals had to be found and, if living, brought back into the herd. After all had been accounted for, the drive could resume, usually with one big difference in the nighttime songs sung to the cattle. "In their next ensuing hymns," writes one historian, "they definitely told the animals what was thought of them."[127]

Herds that had stampeded once tended to do it again. Many cowboys blamed certain steers for being troublemakers, somehow spooking the herd into being more jittery and frightened than usual. These leaders could be dealt with in several ways. Sometimes the steers' eyelids were sewn shut, making them less likely to run at all. The thread would rot over the next few weeks, but by that time the steers had grown more docile.

At other times it was necessary to perform drastic surgery by "kneeing" a troublemaker. A two-inch slit was made in the skin covering one of the animal's kneecaps, and about an inch of cord was removed. The cord would not mend, and if the steer tried to run, it would pitch forward on its head.

But occasionally nothing could be done to change a steer's attitude or lessen its influence over the other animals. Although the cowboys could prevent it from galloping, they might not be able to keep it from scaring the other cattle—from being a "loony." Such a steer was taken out away from the camp and shot, and the men enjoyed a few days of steak dinners on the trail.

Cattle are spooked into stampeding by thunder. A terrible fate awaits the falling cowboy on the right, who will no doubt be trampled to death within seconds.

St. Elmo's Fire and Other Frightening Things

Lightning was one of the most common causes of death on the trail, even when it did not result in a stampede. One cowboy described a storm in Kansas in which lightning "hit the side of those hills and [gouged] out great holes in the earth like a bomb had struck them, and it killed seven or eight cattle in the herd back of us."[128] Another cowboy recalled a night when thirteen steers were struck and killed by bolts of lightning and the rest of the herd stampeded in all directions. Because the plains between Texas and Kansas were so open and flat, the threat of being struck by lightning was especially real.

The moments before an electrical storm brought an eerie feel to the atmosphere. The air seemed thick and heavy, and static electricity made everything seemed charged. On a very dark moonless night, the natural phenomenon known as St. Elmo's fire could be seen. ("Elmo" is a form of the name Erasmus, who was the patron saint of ancient sailors. Sometimes out at sea, blue balls of electricity in the air would play along the masts of ships, frightening the sailors, who dubbed the strange sight "St. Elmo's fire.")

One cowboy remembered a storm on a trail drive in 1877 in which the lightning in the form of blue balls was very visible. "It rolled along the ground . . . then, the most wonderful of all, it settled down on us like a fog. The air smelled of burning sulphur; you could see it," he recalled, "on the horns of the cattle, the ears of our horses, and the brims of our hats. It grew so warm we thought we might burn up with it."[129]

A young wrangler named John Connor recalled how the lightning frightened the horses: "The horses bunched together around me, stuck their heads between their knees and moaned and groaned till I decided the end of time had come. I got down off my horse and lay flat on the ground and tried to die, but could not." [130]

Having seen men struck down in bursts of smoke and flame, cowboys were unashamedly afraid of lightning. One cowboy vividly remembered the first time he saw lightning strike the ground and set the grass on fire. He jerked loose his six-shooter, spurs, and pocket knife, laid them down, and ran away as fast as he could. Cowboys firmly believed that wearing anything metal during an electrical storm was simply asking to die.

Nerves Taut

As the trail drive continued north for months, there usually was tension in the air. The good-natured camaraderie that typically existed among the crew wore thin. It was, writes one expert, "wearisome, grimy business for [the cowboys], who travelled ever in a cloud of dust and the stink of cattle, and heard little but the constant chorus from the crackling of hooves and of ankle joints, from the bellows, lows, and bleats of the trudging animals." [131]

Sleep deprivation also took its toll—getting a few hours of rest at a time, on hard, rocky ground, is not a routine that can be sustained indefinitely. Men on guard duty frequently rubbed tobacco juice under their eyelids because the resulting sting helped keep their eyes open at night.

And when those men came in from guard duty, awakening the cowboys scheduled for the next shift was risky. Writes one historian:

In an attempt to prevent stampedes, cowboys took turns keeping watch throughout the night.

The drudgery of the journey and the constant necessity of alertness against possible stampede and other dangers made nerves so tense that it was unwise to waken any of the men at night by touching him, lest instinctively he draw his pistol. Whoever had need to awaken a man usually either spoke to him or else, from a safe distance, threw pebbles at him. [132]

What broke the tension and ended the irritability was simply the drive's progress. When at last the trail boss announced that they were within a day or two of town—the end of the trail—it was enough to put a smile on the face of even the most surly cowboy. Town was nearby, and the men who had spent the last three or four months living with cattle rejoiced. They wouldn't have to chase, sing to, count, or even look at cows for a while.

Cow Towns and Wild Times

It must have been a joyous feeling for the trail crew, having been months away from civilization, to be nearing town. It would be the end of the drive, the end of that season's work. At last they would be paid for their labor and free to do what they pleased—at least until their money ran out.

Sometimes, however, the cowboys' entrance into town was delayed. If their herd had arrived shortly after other herds, it was necessary to wait a turn at the holding area, and cowboys had to continue to guard the cattle they had herded for months. "It was sheer agony for the men on watch," writes one historian, "to sit in the saddle, grimy as ever, staring at the lights of the distant pleasure palaces and dreaming of what they might be doing."[133]

"Of Course It Was 'Whoop!'"

But eventually the cattle were delivered and sold, and the crew of cowboys paid. Their mood was high and happy, for this is what they had been waiting for. Many turned playful and rowdy as they loped their horses into the main part of town. "There had been a few coyote like whoops of happiness," writes one expert, "and an occasional attempt by a rider either gently to rope the man ahead of him or to discommode his own lateral companion [inconvenience the rider next to him] by means of a sudden sideways pull on the tail of this companion's horse."[134]

Old West historian Philip Rollins defends the rowdiness of the cowboys. After all, he argues:

Young, trained athletes had just completed a drive of perhaps four months of actual riding in the awful dust of the cattle herd, possibly had been delayed for three or four additional months by stock quarantines upon the route. Now they had reached their destination, and their task was done. "Whoop!" Of course it was "Whoop!"[135]

On the trail they had been expected to behave, to follow the rules of the trail boss. In the cow towns of Kansas, however, there were few rules. It seemed that the towns existed for the sheer purpose of making sure cowboys had a good time. The cowboys had money in their pockets—somewhere between $50 and $90. There would be plenty of ways the town would help them spend it all.

Not Much to Look At

The cow town might have seemed like paradise to the cowboy coming off the trail drive, but a closer look would reveal a pretty unimpressive place. There were about fifteen cow towns in Kansas during the trail-driving days of the late nineteenth century, but they all were fairly similar.

Dodge City, Kansas, in 1879 was a typical cow town. Although unimpressive, cowboys thought of such towns as paradise.

None of them had populations exceeding twelve hundred. Of course, this number swelled dramatically when more than a thousand cowboys, ranchers, and cattle buyers overran a town. There were no trees, and the buildings had just one story, although many businesses erected false fronts that gave the impression of two stories. Homes and businesses were built of unpainted pine.

There was no public water supply. People got water from rivers and creeks, with the accompanying risk of disease from water contaminated by germs from cattle manure or garbage. No indoor plumbing was available, so an outhouse sat behind every home, hotel, and restaurant.

The streets were wide and unpaved. Dirt and dust were everywhere, stirred up by the strong prairie winds and horses' hooves. When it rained, everything was muddy. Businesses frequently built pine sidewalks, but boards were often missing; road and sidewalk maintenance was not high on the list of a town's priorities. Barrels of water lined the streets, for everything was made of wood, and fire was a constant danger.

What to Do First?

The most critical need, the cowboy felt, was to get the dust, sweat, and grime of three or four months off his body. A bath in those days meant a visit to the barber, for barbershops usually had a tub in the back room. For 25 cents, a cowboy could have a long, hot soak—soap and afterbath cologne tossed in free.

Afterward he usually treated himself to a shave—"having his face scraped artistic"—and his hair cut—"curried proper." In the days of the Old West, it was stylish for men to have their mustaches blackened and shaped, too.

Another crucial need for every trail drive participant was a new set of clothes. The old ones, grimy and threadbare, were almost never worth saving. After buying new underclothes, a shirt, and a pair of pants from the haberdasher, a cowboy usually visited a

A saloon caters to cowboys off the trail by providing liquor, gambling, and a shave.

"An Institution in the West"

More than any other food, oysters were what cowboys ordered when they went to a restaurant in town. Whether in soup or eaten raw, writes cowboy expert Philip Ashton Rollins in his book, The Cowboy: An Unconventional History of Civilization on the Old-Time Cattle Range, *oysters were popular because they appealed to the cowboy's imagination.*

"As for oysters—Americans of today can have no table pleasure commensurate with that of eating 'cove oysters' on the Western plains fifty years ago. These oysters, a product of Maryland, were packed in sealed cans, each can the size and shape of a brick and decorated with a gaudy picture of a huge bivalve lying on a tiny beach and sprayed by Lilliputian waves. These oysters may have been huge and flabby, may have been poor in quality, may have been wholly ruined by the masses of vinegar, salt, and pepper with which the Western caterer doused them, but they were nectar and ambrosia to the cowboy. Perhaps, after all, they appealed not so much to the palate as to the imagination. They were the only things which could carry to the plains the tang of the ocean, and their eating always was accompanied by much discussion of boats and of the people 'that go down to the sea in ships, that do business in great waters.' They were, to the man whose nostrils breathed only dry-kilned air, what a painting of snow-clad mountains was to the broiling city folk on a midsummer day. Cove oysters were once an institution in the West."

local bootmaker. In Abilene, Texas, a famous cow town, Tom C. McInerney had the finest boot store. For a price extraordinarily low by today's standards—between $12 and $20—a cowboy could walk out with a pair of red-topped, high-heeled boots with tooled lone stars (the symbol of the state) and crescent moons. Boots were available in the Kansas cow towns, as well.

"Cleaning Out a Town"

Smelling sweet and all decked out in their new clothes, the cowboys were ready to "raise a little hell." That meant dancing, hollering, and drinking. As one Wichita newspaper writer observed:

When he feels well (and he always does when full of what he calls "Kansas sheep dip"), the average cowboy is a bad man to handle. Armed to the teeth, well-mounted, and full of their favorite beverage, the cowboys will dash through the principal streets of a town yelling like Comanches. This they call "cleaning out a town."[136]

Such behavior was not popular with the townspeople. One historian writes that "over the entire scene hovered the stern silence of disapproval that emanated from the cattle town's handful of respectable citizens."[137] Cow towns, interestingly, were of two minds on the subject of cowboys.

The problem was not so much the cowboys as the activities that were set up to attract the cowboys when they came to town. For the presence of cowboys and cattle buyers, with their pockets stuffed with money, "attracted honest merchants and professional people," writes one historian, "but they also lured characters with get-rich-quick schemes: gamblers, prostitutes, con-artists, and others seeking something for nothing or for very little effort."[138]

It was these "characters" and the businesses they opened in the cow towns that drew the disapproval of citizens. Yet much as the local residents deplored the drinking, gambling, and prostitution, they needed the revenue from those businesses to thrive. As one Wichita newspaper editor reminded his readers in 1874:

> The taxes are paid by the money received from whiskey sellers [and] gambling halls . . . and thousands of dollars are obtained to further the interests of the town. Wichita flourishes off the cattle business and these evils have to be put up with, at least that is the way a large majority of the people see it.[139]

Cowboys whoop it up with women in a dance hall. Although citizens of cow towns frowned on such behavior, they tolerated it because the cowboys spent money in the small towns.

So the townspeople shook their heads, and probably did a lot of grumbling and complaining, while at the same time collecting hundreds of thousands of dollars in revenue from the cowboys. At least for a while, the cow towns would adopt a "live and let live" attitude.

Saloons and the Devil's Addition

It helped somewhat that towns had a special section reserved for the cowboys and their activities. In Abilene, for example, the collection of saloons, dance halls, and gambling establishments was known as the Devil's Addition. One businessman who disapproved of that part of town claimed that it was well named. "Money and whiskey flowed like water down hill," he complained, "and youth and beauty and womanhood and manhood were wrecked and damned in that valley of perdition."[140]

Cowboys gamble away their earnings during a much-needed rest in town.

The "Big Time"

In his book Cowboys of the Wild West, *Russell Freedman quoted an old cowboy named G.O. Burrows who commented on the cycle of life of the trail cowboy. After 18 or 20 years on the trail, Burrows says, he was not able to save any of his money, but instead spent it in the same ways, each year.*

"I always had the 'big time' when I arrived in good old Santone rigged out with a pair of high-heeled boots and striped breeches, and about $6.30 worth of other clothes. Along about sundown you could find me at Jack Harris' show occupying a front seat and clamoring for the next performance. This 'big time' would last but a few days, however, for I would soon be 'busted' and have to borrow money to get out to the ranch, where I would put in the fall and winter telling about the big things I had seen up north. The next spring I would have the same old trip, the same old things would happen in the same old way, and with the same old wind-up. I put in eighteen or twenty years on the trail, and all I had in the final outcome was the high-heeled boots, the striped pants and about $480 worth of other clothes, so there you are."

Saloons—open twenty-four hours a day—outnumbered the other businesses in town by a 2 to 1 margin. They were dark, smelly places, long and narrow and lit by the dim yellow glow of kerosene lamps. It was hard to tell what time of day it was, for the light inside was always the same. There were brass cuspidors spaced around the saloon, for many patrons chewed tobacco. The floor had a thick coating of sawdust or straw to soak up the spit of those whose aim was less than perfect. Writes one expert, "The blend of tobacco, liquor, straw, horses, kerosene, and human sweat in the summer and the sometimes sizzling spit of tobacco on a hot stove in the fall or early spring left an unforgettable odor, one that many cowboys probably looked forward to on the long trail drives north."[141]

The choice of beverages in saloons was minimal—usually only whiskey and beer. In the early days of the cow town, it was impossible to get shipments of good whiskey from the East, so bartenders frequently mixed their own. They used vats of raw alcohol, colored it brown with tea or coffee, and seasoned it with pepper. Adds one historian, "To give added 'bite,' [the bartender] might toss in a dead rat or snake."[142]

There were gaming tables in the saloons, where cowboys could play poker, faro, keno, and a dice game called chuck-a-luck. There were professional gamblers at the tables, and although cowboys often won some money, it was usually just enough to make them bet more—and lose. Many a cowboy lost every penny he made in the trail drive at saloon gaming tables.

The Galloping Cow and Hambone Jane

One of the biggest attractions in the cowboy section of town was the dance hall. There

"Bendin' an Elbow"

Although many who wrote about cowboys exaggerated when describing the drinking sprees cowboys enjoyed in town after a trail drive, the saloon did play a very real role at the end of the trail drive. As author Ramon Adams writes in his article "Bendin' an Elbow," quoted in Lon Tinkle's and Allen Maxwell's anthology The Cowboy Reader, *cowboys used a unique style in describing saloons and the whiskey served there.*

"The quality of liquor served in some of the frontier saloons would 'eat its way plum to your boot soles.' Hoot Gilroy, complaining of such liquor, told the barkeep that he 'forgot to strain this stuff to get out the tobaccer leaves.' Muley Metcalf once stated to a barkeep in Silver City that 'you should a-been a snake charmer, judgin' from the likker you're shovin' across the mahogany,' and Bill Pitman told another in Cheyenne that he 'might be the best bar-dog that ever waved a bar-rag, but I don't want you spittin' tobaccer juice in the barrel to make it pleasant to the taste.' At another time Stormy Morse described such whiskey as 'a brand o' booze that a man could git drunk on and be shot through the brain and it wouldn't kill 'im till he sobered up,' and Speed Carlow claimed emphatically that 'you couldn't gargle that brand o' hooch without annexin' a few queer animals.'

In speaking of low dives, the cowboy artist Charles Russell once described such a place as 'a dive that made the other dives look like a kindergarten or a ladies' finishin' school,' and Calico Starnes told of one town on the Mexican border 'where a skunk would be ashamed to meet his own mother.'"

Cowboys step up to have a drink in a cow town saloon.

were lots of women there, ready and willing to show the cowboys a good time. The women—many of them only teenagers—were known by various titles: "soiled doves," "calico queens," "frail sisters," and "sporting women." They drank and entertained cowboys in their rooms, which tended to anger the townspeople. Their disapproval was expressed by one newspaper editorial writer: "Here [in the saloons and dance halls] you may see young girls not over 16 drinking whiskey, smoking cigars, cursing and swearing until one almost loses the respect they should have for the weaker sex. I heard one of their townsmen say he didn't believe there were a dozen virtuous women in town."[143]

The women went by "stage names" that were easy for the cowboys to remember. Some typical "soiled doves" in the cow towns had names like Cuttin' Lil Slasher, Wicked Alice, the Galloping Cow, Hambone Jane, Peg-Leg Annie, Irish Molly, Kitty Kirl, and Squirrel Tooth Alice—named for the pet squirrel she constantly carried around.

"All the Girls Acted Glad to See You"

Whatever the townspeople thought of them, the "soiled doves" *did* add energy and excitement to the dance hall. Remembers one cowboy:

I walked up to the dance halls and looked in. What a sight to anyone, the prettiest gals from all over the world, dressed like a million dollars, was all there. If you did not come in to dance, they would grab you and pull you in, whether you wanted to dance or not. All the girls acted glad to see you. Round after round of drinks, then all would dance.[144]

Perhaps it might have seemed out of character, but many cowboys, once they got to town, did enjoy dancing, and did not seem to worry that their version of dancing was a little strange. One man who spent time in Abilene's dance halls describes it:

The cowboy enters the dance with a peculiar zest, not stopping to divest himself of his sombrero, spurs, or pistols, but just as he dismounts off his cow-pony, so he goes into the dance. A more odd, not to say comical sight, is not often seen than the dancing cowboy; with the front of his sombrero lifted at an angle of fully 45 degrees; his huge spurs jingling at every stop or motion; his revolvers flapping up and down like a retreating sheep's tail.[145]

Musical shows were popular in some of the larger cow towns. Women in elaborate costumes would sing and dance, much to the delight of the cowboys. Besides whistling and cheering, audiences often showed their approval by tossing silver dollars at the stage. One historian writes of a cowboy who "became so enthralled at the way 'The Last Kiss My Darling Mother Gave' was described in coyote tremolo [terribly bad singing] by a blonde soprano, that he hurled a twenty-dollar gold piece, which, accidentally hitting the songstress behind the ear, knocked her senseless."[146]

"Hell Is Now in Session"

Given the drinking and gambling that went on in cow towns, it is not surprising that crime was a problem. The cow towns were basically frontier outposts, far from the organization enjoyed by towns in eastern Kansas. Those

Cowboys stampede through the street, firing their six-shooters in the air and threatening local inhabitants.

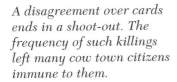

A disagreement over cards ends in a shoot-out. The frequency of such killings left many cow town citizens immune to them.

who settled in places like Wichita and Dodge City (to name only two of the fifteen) were usually far too busy establishing businesses or farms to think about enforcing the law.

The result was often chaos. The antics of the cowboys, gamblers, and others became wilder and wilder, for there was no one to levy fines or impose jail sentences. Sometimes the trouble was merely noise and rowdiness—lots of horses racing up and down the wide streets of town, six-shooters being fired at the sky, at

signs, or even at the water barrels that lined the sidewalks. "We like to get up a little racket now and then," explained one cowboy, "but it's all in play."[147]

However, the cow towns attracted some rough characters, too, and the trouble often turned ugly. Drunken brawls sometimes ended in homicide; a man caught cheating at cards might be gunned down. Some of the towns' inhabitants seemed to take the murders and shootings in their stride.

One man saw a discussion at the bar of a Dodge City saloon end when a man drew his six-shooter and fired into another man's ear, nearly blowing his head off his body. One of the dance hall girls standing nearby became excited at the sight of the blood. According to this witness, the girl "put the palms of her hands down into the blood that was running on the floor, jumped up and down and hollered, 'Cock-a-doodle-do!' Then she held her hands up and clapped them in front of her, splattering the blood all over her white dress." Said the observer, "I just closed the door and went back to bed."[148]

Fading Out of Town

In many instances, desperate citizens formed town councils and made rules—no public drunkenness, and especially no guns within the town limits. To enforce the laws, towns hired marshals and other peace officers. Some "took one look at the rip-roaring main street and hopped the midnight train out again."[149] Many stayed, however, and had varying degrees of success in fighting the criminals who operated in the towns. The names of some of these men have become legendary: Wyatt Earp and Bat Masterson in Dodge City; James Butler "Wild Bill" Hickock in Abilene. Because of their efforts—and to a greater extent, the support of a growing population of "decent" citizens—the cow towns gradually became less violent.

And what of the cowboy? Within a few days of coming to town, he was usually broke. As one historian writes, "The members of the party, in the order of their entering insolvency, made announcement of their intended departure."[150] A few, deciding that the life was too difficult, might vow to try some other line of work, perhaps going "back

Wild Bill Hickock became marshal of Abilene, Texas. He was hired by citizens of the town to control cowboys' rough behavior.

North" or "back East." But most saddled up any horse they could buy for a few dollars—or better yet, borrow—and headed back to Texas. They had, as Philip Rollins writes, "come into the town boldly, but they faded out of it."[151]

The End of the Trail

By 1890 the era of the cowboy had passed. The open range was a thing of the past, as were most of the men who had depended on it for their livelihood. Many factors caused the end of the open-range cattle business, not least of which was the westward push of the railroad. This was ironic, for that same westward push had sparked the expansion of the cattle industry in the first place.

As the railroad workers (known as "gandy dancers," because of their rhythmic movements in working with tools made by the Gandy Company of Chicago) laid rails stretching farther west, more people streamed into areas that had been frontier. That brought civilization, and with civilization came farmers, who shared the feelings of their peers in eastern and central Kansas about the Texas longhorns: They wanted the longhorns out of Kansas, out of their territory.

The Texas fever was still as deadly, and the only way to control the ticks that carried the disease was to restrict the movement of Texas cattle in Kansas. And so with the quarantine line moving westward, like the railroads, trail drives ended in new cow towns, far from the angry farmers and their shotguns.

Cold-Weather Cows and Beef Bonanzas

Even though the new restrictions were an irritant and a bother to the Texas ranchers and their trail crews, business was still good.

Hundreds of thousands of cattle were being driven north from Texas each year, and the nation was enjoying beef as a regular part of its diet. Business was booming.

Part of the success of the cattle business was due to the expansion of "cattle country"—once thought of as pretty much limited to Texas. By the 1870s and 1880s, cattle were being raised throughout the northern Great Plains, too, in places like the Montana, Wyoming, and Dakota territories. The cattle were a new breed—a cross between the longhorns and the heavier,

Cowboys drive cattle out of the stockyards in Chicago to slaughter.

"The Last Longhorn"

In his book The Cowboy and His Interpreters, *Douglas Branch quotes a well-known cowboy song called "The Last Longhorn." Its melancholy tone reflects the sadness cowboys felt at the passing of the age of the open range.*

An ancient long-horned bovine
Lay dying by the river;
There was lack of vegetation
And the cold winds made him shiver;
A cowboy sat beside him,
With sadness in his face,
To see his final passing—
The last of a noble race.

The ancient eunuch struggled
And raised his aching head,
Saying, "I care not to linger
When all my friends are dead.
These Jerseys and these Holsteins,
They are no friends of mine;
They belong to the nobility
Who live across the brine.

"I remember back in the Seventies,
Full many summers past,
There was grass and water plenty,
But it was too good to last.
I little dreamed what would happen
Some twenty summers since,
When the nester came with his wife, his kids,
His dogs and his barbed-wire fence."

And the cowboy rose up sadly
And mounted his cayuse,
Saying, "The time has come when longhorns
And their cowboys are no use!"
And while gazing sadly backward
Upon the dead bovine,
His bronc stepped in a dog-hole
And fell and broke his spine.

short-horned Herefords. These cattle were hardy and able to withstand cold winters—something the longhorns could not do. Texas ranchers learned this the hard way in 1871, when tens of thousands of longhorns died while awaiting a buyer in Kansas. Snow had come unseasonably early that fall, and the longhorns, unused to pawing the snow to find grass underneath, either froze or starved.

A rancher with the new "cold-weather cows," as cowboys jokingly called them, had what seemed like unlimited grazing lands for his cattle. And because millions of buffalo had been all but exterminated by hunters, the cattle had no rivals for the rich green grass that blanketed the prairies.

The rising prices ranchers were getting for their cattle encouraged more and more people to enter the business. Many came from cities in the East, using their capital to invest in huge parcels of land on the plains, with huge herds to go along with that land. Others came from farther away— Ireland, Scotland, England, and other European nations.

Some of the excitement was fueled by exaggerated and misleading accounts of life in America, and especially of the supposedly risk-free business of raising cattle. One book, *The Beef Bonanza: or How to Get Rich on the Plains,* by James S. Brisbin, claimed, "I believe that all the flocks and herds in the world could find ample pasturage on these unoccupied plains and the mountain slopes beyond."[152] According to Brisbin's mathematics, a cattle rancher could double an investment of $100,000 in just five years.

"The Devil's Hat Band"

The use of barbed wire fencing had a strong influence on the cattle business during this boom period. Invented in the early 1870s by an Illinois farmer named Joseph Glidden, the wire fencing with twists of sharp strands of wire spaced across it was a cheap alternative to stone fences and fences with wooden bars.

As more and more people took up cattle ranching and farming in the West, good grazing land and watering holes became even more precious than ever. With barbed wire fencing, ranchers or farmers could easily

With the increased mobility the railroad allowed ranchers, and the invention of barbed wire, ranches could be set up near towns, eliminating the need for cattle drives.

enclose their land to protect their fields, or to keep their livestock from wandering.

However, barbed wire fences were misused by many—especially wealthy ranchers who could afford extra miles of fencing to connect public lands to their own, giving them additional water and grass for their herds. This practice infuriated nearby ranchers, who suddenly found themselves without

Small farmers, masked against recognition, cut the wire which cattlemen have used to fence off their water supply. Such tactics did not work, however, and the free range became a series of ranches.

access to water or additional grazing land for their cattle. Disputes and fence-cutting fights often ended in violence.

As the once-open ranges of the Great Plains became crisscrossed with wire, angry ranchers complained that the fencing was going to change the whole industry. Cowboys worried that their way of life would be forever gone. They wished that the fellow who had invented the stuff "had it all wound around him in a ball and the ball rolled into hell."[153]

A popular song among cowboys was about barbed wire:

> They say that heaven is a free range land,
> Goodbye, goodbye, O fare you well;
> But it's barbed wire fence for the devil's hat band;
> And barbed wire blankets down in hell.[154]

One Texas trail driver agreed with this sentiment when he wrote:

> These fellows from Ohio, Indiana, and other northern and western states—the "bone and sinew of the country," as the politicians call them—have made farms, enclosed pastures, and fenced in water-holes until you can't rest; and I say, Damn such bone and sinew! They are the ruin of the country, and have everlastingly, eternally, now and forever, destroyed the best grazing land in the world. The range country . . . was never intended for raising farm-truck. . . . I am sick . . . when I think of onions and Irish potatoes growing where mustang ponies should be exercising, and four-year-old steers should be getting ripe for market. Fences, sir, are the curse of the country![155]

The Knockout Punches

Nature delivered the series of disasters that proved to be the end of the "beef bonanza." The first was a drought beginning in the early 1880s that seriously affected the grazing land on the plains. The temperatures were hot and the cloudless skies held not even a faint hope of rain.

The green grass on which the herds had depended was turning into straw. Since the cattle population was growing at such a high rate, the grass was already taking a beating, say historians, for cows were much harder on the grass than the millions of buffalo had been. Writer Albert Marrin explains the difference:

> Buffalo herds would eat the grass, drop their chips, and move on to fresh pasture. Their manure fertilized the soil, and their hooves broke the ground, letting in air and moisture. Cattle are different. They bite off the grass at ground level, then eat the new shoots, never giving the grass a chance to recover.[156]

As grass died, the soil turned to powdery dust and blew away. Creek beds and other watering spots dried up. Cattle went blind, suffering agonizing deaths by the tens of thousands. Prairie fires were frequent on the dry grass. Cowboys, having no water supply to extinguish the blazes, were sometimes forced to kill cattle, split them in half along their backbones, and drag the corpses around the fire's perimeter to stop the progress of the flames.

The Die-Up

If desperate cattle ranchers thought things could not get worse, they were very wrong.

A blizzard causes cattle to slowly freeze to death during the terrible winter of 1886. Millions of open-range cattle died.

The winter of 1886 was more terrible than anyone could have believed possible, with record-setting snowfalls and below-zero temperatures. Historians say that whole families froze in their homes in Montana and the Dakotas, for they had no fuel.

The loss to the cattle herds was appalling. "Millions of open range cattle were scattered for miles," writes one expert, "dead or dying, heaped against the . . . fences of homesteaders, frozen stiff as statues in solid drifts, drowned in the air pockets of snow-blanketed rivers."[157] Mad with hunger, skeletal cattle stormed into the streets of Great Falls, Montana. They uprooted young trees to get at the roots and branches; they fought over scraps of garbage found in the snow. In the Dakotas, townspeople reported cattle desperately ate the tar paper from the sides of shacks until they died.

When the storms were finally over, the shocked cowboys and ranch owners surveyed the extent of the disaster. In Dodge City, the newspaper gave this grim report:

Within a few miles of here, no less than five hundred cattle have drifted to the river, where they perished in attempting to cross, or drifted up to fences, where they remained until frozen to death. A gentleman from a ranch south of here reports seeing cattle on his way up that were still standing on their feet frozen to death.[158]

As the warm winds of spring began melting the snow drifts, ranchers were met with gruesome sights, such as hundreds of dead steers damming the rivers, "rolling over and over in the churning current, bobbing up and down on the crests of the flood waters."[159] Other ranchers recalled seeing dead steers high in the branches of a tree, where they had struggled through drifts to get at the bark.

The winter of 1886, when more than a million cattle perished, was referred to—and still is today—as the Die-Up. Besides the astonishing loss of life, there was financial

The remains of a longhorn steer that died during the winter of 1886. Cattle were not the only casualties; whole families froze to death as well.

Cattle are loaded onto railcars for shipment to Abilene. The advent of the railroad brought an end to cattle drives and to the cowboy lifestyle.

ruin for many ranchers. Those who had enough capital saved to survive in the business vowed that there had to be changes. Said one rancher who lost 66 percent of his stock, "I never wanted to own again an animal that I couldn't feed or shelter."[160]

"Wherever They Are Is Where I Want to Go"

By the 1890s the cattle industry had been drastically changed. Because the railroads now went all the way to Texas, long trail drives were unnecessary. There were no more open ranges, and cowboys spent more of their time doing chores they once had scoffed at—building and repairing fences, fixing windmills that pumped water for the enclosed herds, and mowing hay.

Some cowboys, disgusted by what was happening, went farther west or into Canada to find trail work. But the days of the cowboy—the real cowboy who drove herds from Texas for months at a time—was a thing of the past. The only trail driving consisted of moving herds from a holding pen to a cattle car. True, there were no stampedes, no long nights without sleep. But neither were there trips to town, the good times talking around the fire, or singing lonely ballads to the herds.

Teddy Blue Abbott wrote sadly about the life he had enjoyed as a cowboy, and mourned the loss of the friends he had known:

> I believe I would know an old cowboy in hell with his hide burnt off. It's the way they stand and walk and talk. . . . Only a few of us are left now and they are scattered from Texas to Canada. The rest have left the wagon and gone ahead across the big divide, looking for a new range. I hope they find good water and plenty of grass. But wherever they are is where I want to go.[161]

Notes

Introduction: An American Fixture

1. Russell Freedman, *Cowboys of the Wild West.* New York: Clarion Books, 1985.
2. William W. Savage Jr., *Cowboy Life: Reconstructing an American Myth.* Norman: University of Oklahoma Press, 1975.
3. Jack Weston, *The Real American Cowboy.* New York: Schocken Books, 1985.
4. Weston, *The Real American Cowboy.*
5. Quoted in Weston, *The Real American Cowboy.*

Chapter 1: The Roots of the American Cowboy

6. Muñoz Camargo, quoted in David Dary, *Cowboy Culture: A Saga of Five Centuries.* Lawrence: University Press of Kansas, 1981.
7. Albert Marrin, *Cowboys, Indians, and Gunfighters.* New York: Atheneum, 1993.
8. Richard W. Slatta, *Cowboys of the Americas.* New Haven, CT: Yale University Press, 1990.
9. Marrin, *Cowboys, Indians, and Gunfighters.*
10. Dary, *Cowboy Culture.*
11. Dary, *Cowboy Culture.*
12. Dary, *Cowboy Culture.*
13. Dary, *Cowboy Culture.*
14. Quoted in Slatta, *Cowboys of the Americas.*
15. Marrin, *Cowboys, Indians, and Gunfighters.*
16. Quoted in Don Ward, *Cowboys and Cattle Country.* New York: American Heritage, 1961.
17. Marrin, *Cowboys, Indians, and Gunfighters.*
18. Quoted in Ward, *Cowboys and Cattle Country.*
19. Ward, *Cowboys and Cattle Country.*

Chapter 2: The Masters of the Range

20. Quoted in Edward S. Barnard, ed., *Story of the American West.* Pleasantville, NY: Reader's Digest, 1977.
21. William H. Forbis, *The Cowboys.* New York: Time-Life Books, 1973.
22. Quoted in Forbis, *The Cowboys.*
23. Quoted in Barnard, *Story of the American West.*
24. Quoted in Forbis, *The Cowboys.*
25. Philip Ashton Rollins, *The Cowboy: An Unconventional History of Civilization on the Old-Time Cattle Range.* Albuquerque: University of New Mexico Press, 1922.
26. Quoted in Forbis, *The Cowboys.*
27. Quoted in Rollins, *The Cowboy.*
28. Rollins, *The Cowboy.*
29. Rollins, *The Cowboy.*
30. Marrin, *Cowboys, Indians, and Gunfighters.*
31. Rollins, *The Cowboy.*
32. Marrin, *Cowboys, Indians, and Gunfighters.*
33. Forbis, *The Cowboys.*
34. Rollins, *The Cowboy.*
35. Rollins, *The Cowboy.*
36. Quoted in Slatta, *Cowboys of the Americas.*
37. Forbis, *The Cowboys.*
38. Quoted in Stan Hoig, *The Humor of the American Cowboy.* Caldwell, ID: Caxton Printers, 1958.
39. John James Callison, *Bill Jones of Paradise Valley, Oklahoma: His Life and*

Adventures for Over Forty Years in the Great Southwest. Chicago: M.A. Donohue, 1914.

40. Forbis, *The Cowboys.*
41. Quoted in Slatta, *Cowboys of the Americas.*
42. Quoted in Slatta, *Cowboys of the Americas.*
43. Quoted in Weston, *The Real American Cowboy.*
44. Quoted in Weston, *The Real American Cowboy.*

Chapter 3: All a Cowboy Needs . . .

45. Forbis, *The Cowboys.*
46. Quoted in Douglas Kent Hall, *Working Cowboys.* New York: Holt, Rinehart, and Winston, 1984.
47. Rollins, *The Cowboy.*
48. Rollins, *The Cowboy.*
49. Quoted in Douglas Branch, *The Cowboy and His Interpreters.* New York: D. Appleton, 1926.
50. Dee Brown, *Trail Driving Days.* New York: Charles Scribner's Sons, 1952.
51. Forbis, *The Cowboys.*
52. Rollins, *The Cowboy.*
53. Quoted in Branch, *The Cowboy and His Interpreters.*
54. Quoted in Rollins, *The Cowboy.*
55. Branch, *The Cowboy and His Interpreters.*
56. David H. Murdoch, *Cowboy.* New York: Knopf, 1993.
57. E.C. Abbott and Helen Huntington, *We Pointed Them North.* Norman: University of Oklahoma Press, 1939.
58. Rollins, *The Cowboy.*
59. Abbott and Huntington, *We Pointed Them North.*
60. Quoted in Branch, *The Cowboy and His Interpreters.*
61. Rollins, *The Cowboy.*
62. Rollins, *The Cowboy.*
63. Marrin, *Cowboys, Indians, and Gunfighters.*
64. Quoted in Branch, *The Cowboy and His Interpreters.*
65. John H. Culley, *Cattle, Horses, and Men of the Western Range.* Los Angeles: Ward Ritchie Press, 1940.

Chapter 4: From Brushpopping to Roundups

66. Rollins, *The Cowboy.*
67. Joe B. Frantz and Julian Ernest Choate Jr., *The American Cowboy: The Myth and the Reality.* Norman: University of Oklahoma Press, 1955.
68. Frantz and Choate, *The American Cowboy.*
69. Will James, *Cowboys North and South.* New York: Charles Scribner's Sons, 1924.
70. Don Worcester, *The Chisholm Trail: High Road of the Cattle Kingdom.* Lincoln: University of Nebraska Press, 1980.
71. Quoted in Brown, *Trail Driving Days.*
72. Worcester, *The Chisholm Trail.*
73. Brown, *Trail Driving Days.*
74. Worcester, *The Chisholm Trail.*
75. Quoted in Brown, *Trail Driving Days.*
76. Worcester, *The Chisholm Trail.*
77. James, *Cowboys North and South.*
78. Worcester, *The Chisholm Trail.*
79. Worcester, *The Chisholm Trail.*
80. Forbis, *The Cowboys.*
81. Branch, *The Cowboy and His Interpreters.*
82. Branch, *The Cowboy and His Interpreters.*
83. Branch, *The Cowboy and His Interpreters.*
84. Branch, *The Cowboy and His Interpreters.*

85. Forbis, *The Cowboys.*
86. Quoted in Forbis, *The Cowboys.*
87. Brown, *Trail Driving Days.*
88. Brown, *Trail Driving Days.*
89. Quoted in Forbis, *The Cowboys.*
90. Dary, *Cowboy Culture.*
91. Branch, *The Cowboy and His Interpreters.*
92. Dary, *Cowboy Culture.*
93. Branch, *The Cowboy and His Interpreters.*
94. Branch, *The Cowboy and His Interpreters.*

Chapter 5: Starting Up the Trail

95. Branch, *The Cowboy and His Interpreters.*
96. Branch, *The Cowboy and His Interpreters.*
97. Branch, *The Cowboy and His Interpreters.*
98. Ramon F. Adams, *Come an' Get It: The Story of the Old Cowboy Cook.* Norman: University of Oklahoma Press, 1952.
99. Forbis, *The Cowboys.*
100. Ward, *Cowboys and Cattle Country.*
101. Abbott and Huntington, *We Pointed Them North.*
102. Rollins, *The Cowboy.*
103. Quoted in Forbis, *The Cowboys.*
104. Adams, *Come an' Get It.*
105. Adams, *Come an' Get It.*
106. Adams, *Come an' Get It.*
107. Adams, *Come an' Get It.*
108. Adams, *Come an' Get It.*
109. Adams, *Come an' Get It.*
110. Adams, *Come an' Get It.*
111. Brown, *Trail Driving Days.*

Chapter 6: Trouble on the Trail

112. Quoted in Forbis, *The Cowboys.*
113. Branch, *The Cowboy and His Interpreters.*

114. Quoted in Branch, *The Cowboy and His Interpreters.*
115. Andy Adams, *Trail Drive: A True Narrative of Cowboy Life from Andy Adams' "Log of a Cowboy."* New York: Holiday House, 1965.
116. Adams, *Trail Drive.*
117. Quoted in Branch, *The Cowboy and His Interpreters.*
118. Quoted in Worcester, *The Chisholm Trail.*
119. Abbott and Huntington, *We Pointed Them North.*
120. Quoted in Brown, *Trail Driving Days.*
121. Rollins, *The Cowboy.*
122. Quoted in Forbis, *The Cowboys.*
123. Forbis, *The Cowboys.*
124. Branch, *The Cowboy and His Interpreters.*
125. Rollins, *The Cowboy.*
126. Abbott and Huntington, *We Pointed Them North.*
127. Rollins, *The Cowboy.*
128. Quoted in Forbis, *The Cowboys.*
129. Quoted in Forbis, *The Cowboys.*
130. Quoted in Forbis, *The Cowboys.*
131. Rollins, *The Cowboy.*
132. Rollins, *The Cowboy.*

Chapter 7: Cow Towns and Wild Times

133. Forbis, *The Cowboys.*
134. Rollins, *The Cowboy.*
135. Rollins, *The Cowboy.*
136. Quoted in Dary, *Cowboy Culture.*
137. Forbis, *The Cowboys.*
138. Dary, *Cowboy Culture.*
139. Quoted in Dary, *Cowboy Culture.*
140. Quoted in Forbis, *The Cowboys.*
141. Dary, *Cowboy Culture.*
142. Marrin, *Cowboys, Indians, and Gunfighters.*
143. Quoted in Forbis, *The Cowboys.*

144. Quoted in Brown, *Trail Driving Days*.
145. Quoted in Dary, *Cowboy Culture*.
146. Rollins, *The Cowboy*.
147. Quoted in Marrin, *Cowboys, Indians, and Gunfighters*.
148. Quoted in Marrin, *Cowboys, Indians, and Gunfighters*.
149. Quoted in Forbis, *The Cowboys*.
150. Rollins, *The Cowboy*.
151. Rollins, *The Cowboy*.

Conclusion: The End of the Trail

152. Quoted in Ward, *Cowboys and Cattle Country*.
153. Quoted in Ward, *Cowboys and Cattle Country*.
154. Quoted in Marrin, *Cowboys, Indians, and Gunfighters*.
155. Quoted in Dary, *Cowboy Culture*.
156. Marrin, *Cowboys, Indians, and Gunfighters*.
157. Brown, *Trail Driving Days*.
158. Quoted in Brown, *Trail Driving Days*.
159. Brown, *Trail Driving Days*.
160. Quoted in Brown, *Trail Driving Days*.
161. Abbott and Huntington, *We Pointed Them North*.Abbott, Teddy Blue, 40 42, 67, 78, 99

For Further Reading

Andy Adams, *Trail Drive: A True Narrative of Cowboy Life from Andy Adams' "Log of a Cowboy."* New York: Holiday House, 1965. Excellent reading. Good description of a cattle stampede.

Usher L. Burdick, *Some of the Old-Time Cowmen of the Great West.* Baltimore: Wirth Brothers, 1957. Excellent, readable sections on some of the dangers of the long trail drive.

Mike Flanagan, *Out West.* New York: Harry N. Abrams, 1987. Good section on the derivation of words from the Old West.

Bart McDowell, *The American Cowboy in Life and Legend.* Washington, DC: National Geographic Society, 1972. Interesting text, excellent color photographs.

Robert H. Miller, *Reflections of a Black Cowboy,* Book One: *Cowboys.* Englewood Cliffs, NJ: Silver Burdett Press, 1991. Highly readable text telling the stories of African-American heroes in the Old West.

James C. Shaw, *North from Texas: Incidents in the Early Life of a Range Cowman in Texas, Dakota, and Wyoming, 1852–1883.* Evanston, IL: Branding Iron Press, 1952. Excellent section on trail drives.

Lon Tinkle and Allen Maxwell, eds., *The Cowboy Reader.* New York: Longmans, Green, 1959. Well-organized anthology of chapters of some of the best-known cowboy journals.

Charles Zurhorst, *The First Cowboys and Those Who Followed.* New York: Abelard-Schuman, 1973. Good section on first American "cowboys" during the time of the American Revolution.

Works Consulted

Ramon F. Adams, *Come an' Get It: The Story of the Old Cowboy Cook*. Norman: University of Oklahoma Press, 1952. One of the most interesting accounts of a cook's role on the trail drive. Well written; lots of detail.

Edward S. Barnard, ed., *Story of the American West*. Pleasantville, NY: Reader's Digest, 1977. A broad overview of the settling of the west.

Douglas Branch, *The Cowboy and His Interpreters*. New York: D. Appleton, 1926. Very readable. Good bibliography.

Dee Brown, *Trail Driving Days*. New York: Charles Scribner's Sons, 1952. Excellent photographs, and a very good chapter dealing with the Die-Up.

John James Callison, *Bill Jones of Paradise Valley, Oklahoma: His Life and Adventures for Over Forty Years in the Great Southwest*. Chicago: M.A. Donohue, 1914. Interesting reading, with good insights into the character of the American cowboy.

John H. Culley, *Cattle, Horses, and Men of the Western Range*. Los Angeles: Ward Ritchie Press, 1940. A good firsthand account of life on the range in the late nineteenth century.

David Dary, *Cowboy Culture: A Saga of Five Centuries*. Lawrence: University Press of Kansas, 1981. Well-researched account of the life of the cowboy; excellent notes.

William H. Forbis, *The Cowboys*. New York: Time-Life Books, 1973. Excellent reading, good section on the cow towns of Kansas. Helpful photographs.

Joe B. Frantz and Julian Ernest Choate Jr., *The American Cowboy: The Myth and the Reality*. Norman: University of Oklahoma Press, 1955. Somewhat difficult reading, but excellent bibliography.

Russell Freedman, *Cowboys of the Wild West*. New York: Clarion Books, 1985. Easy-reading overview of the era of the Old West. Good black-and-white photographs.

Douglas Kent Hall, *Working Cowboys*. New York: Holt, Rinehart, and Winston, 1984. Interviews with modern cowboys, who sound very much like those of the Old West. Good photographs.

Stan Hoig, *The Humor of the American Cowboy*. Caldwell, ID: Caxton Printers, 1958. Highly readable collection of anecdotes from trail drives to bunkhouse living.

Will James, *Cowboys North and South*. New York: Charles Scribner's Sons, 1924. Written in colloquial "cowboy-ese"; good section on cattle rustlers.

Albert Marrin, *Cowboys, Indians, and Gunfighters*. New York: Atheneum, 1993. One of the most readable of the authors; excellent illustrations and photographs.

David H. Murdoch, *Cowboy*. New York: Knopf, 1993. Superb color photographs and captions showing equipment and dress of cowboys.

Philip Ashton Rollins, *The Cowboy: An Unconventional History of Civilization on the Old-Time Cattle Range*. Albuquerque: University of New Mexico Press, 1922. Interesting sections on cowboy apparel and use of horses.

William W. Savage Jr., *Cowboy Life: Reconstructing an American Myth*. Norman: University of Oklahoma Press, 1975. A scholarly study of cowboy life.

Richard W. Slatta, *Cowboys of the Americas.* New Haven, CT: Yale University Press, 1990. A very readable history of the cowboy in North and South America. Excellent photographs.

Don Ward, *Cowboys and Cattle Country.* New York: American Heritage, 1961. Well-illustrated book, with an excellent section on the first ranchers in Texas.

Jack Weston, *The Real American Cowboy.* New York: Schocken Books, 1985. A look at the cowboy as he was viewed by the media; indicates how such a view has blurred the real American cowboy. Good notes; very readable style.

Don Worcester, *The Chisholm Trail: High Road of the Cattle Kingdom.* Lincoln: University of Nebraska Press, 1980. Excellent chapter on the trail boss and his duties.

Index

Picture Credits

Cover photo by Stock Montage, Inc.

Archive Photos/American Stock, 93

The Bettmann Archive, 6, 27, 29, 34, 36, 43, 54, 84, 94

Culver Pictures, Inc., 9, 92 (top)

National Archives, 22

Peter Newark's Western Americana, 8, 11, 14, 15, 16, 17 (both), 18, 20, 24, 25, 26, 28, 32, 37, 38, 39, 40, 41, 44, 45, 47, 48, 50, 51, 52, 55, 56, 57, 59, 61, 62, 63, 64 (both), 65, 67, 69, 72, 74, 76, 78, 80, 83, 86 (both), 88 (both), 90, 92 (bottom), 96 (both), 98 (both), 99

About the Author

Gail B. Stewart received her undergraduate degree from Gustavus Adolphus College in St. Peter, Minnesota. She did her graduate work in English, linguistics, and curriculum study at the College of St. Thomas and the University of Minnesota. Stewart taught English and reading for more than ten years.

She has written over forty-eight books for young people, including a six-part series called *Living Spaces*. She has written several books for Lucent Books including *Drug Trafficking* and *Acid Rain*.

Stewart and her husband live in Minneapolis with their three sons, two dogs, and a cat. She enjoys reading (especially children's books) and playing tennis.